MORE
HOLY
HILARITY

MORE HOLY HILARITY

Inspirational Wit and Cartoons

Cal and Rose Samra

CARMEL • NEW YORK 10512

THIS GUIDEPOSTS EDITION IS PUBLISHED BY SPECIAL ARRANGEMENT WITH THE
FELLOWSHIP OF MERRY CHRISTIANS, INC.

ISBN 1-57856-282-1

For information about membership in the Fellowship of Merry Christians,
including a subscription to *The Joyful Noiseletter,* please call toll-free 1-800-877-2757,
or write to Fellowship of Merry Christians, P.O. Box 895, Portage, MI 49081-0895.
FMC's catalog offers a variety of prints and Christian humor resources.
E-mail: JoyfulNZ@aol.com. Visit FMC's Web site: http://www.joyfulnoiseletter.com.

Unless otherwise stated, all Scripture quotations are taken from *The Living Bible*
copyright © 1971. Used by permission of Tyndale House Publishers, Inc., Wheaton,
Illinois 60189. All rights reserved. Scripture quotations marked (NIV) are taken from
the *Holy Bible, New International Version*®. NIV® Copyright © 1973, 1978, 1984 by
International Bible Society. Used by permission of Zondervan Publishing House.
All rights reserved. Scriptures marked (NASB) are taken from the *New American
Standard Bible*®. © Copyright The Lockman Foundation 1960, 1962, 1963, 1968,
1971, 1972, 1973, 1975, 1977, 1995. Used by permission. Scripture quotations
marked (NKJV) are taken from the *New King James Version.* Copyright © 1982 by
Thomas Nelson, Inc. Used by permission. All rights reserved. Scripture quotations
marked (TEV) are from the *Today's English Version* — Second Edition. Copyright
© 1992 by American Bible Society. Used by permission. Scripture quotations marked
(TJB) are taken from *The Jerusalem Bible* (Reader's Edition) © 1966, 1967 and 1968 by
Darton, Longman & Todd, Ltd. and Doubleday & Company, Inc. Scripture quotations
marked (NJB) are taken from *The New Jerusalem Bible* © 1985 by Darton, Longman
& Todd, Ltd. and Doubleday & Company, Inc. Scripture quotations marked (KJV) are
taken from the *King James Version* (KJV)

Library of Congress Cataloging-in-Publication Data
More holy hilarity : a book of inspirational humor and cartoons /
    [compiled by] Cal and Rose Samra. — 1st ed.
                    p.   cm.
        Includes indexes.
        ISBN 1-57856-282-1
        1. Christian life Humor. 2. Christianity Humor. 3. Church Humor.
    I. Samra, Cal. II. Samra, Rose.
    PN6231.C35M67   1999
    230'.002'07—dc21   99-33694
                                                                CIP
Printed in the United States of America

To

the marvelous cartoonists

of The Joyful Noiseletter

Contents

ⓖ

What is more joyful than the joy of a saint,

what more happy than the happiness of a believer?

— CHARLES SPURGEON

Never let anything so fill you with sorrow as to make you forget

for one moment the joy of Christ risen.

— MOTHER TERESA

Introduction

⊚

For fourteen years, *The Joyful Noiseletter*, the monthly newsletter of the Fellowship of Merry Christians, has been bringing joy and laughter into America's sanctuaries.

We have tried to demonstrate that faith can be fun and that humor can be healing.

We are gratified that so many pastors of all denominations have been able to wake up and cheer up their congregations with the jokes, anecdotes, stories, and cartoons in *The Joyful Noiseletter*. We are also thankful that so many health professionals have found the materials useful in boosting the spirits of their patients.

We thank all of the members of the Fellowship of Merry Christians who contributed to this book. Acknowledgments for larger contributions follow. We are especially grateful to the gifted cartoonists who contributed to this book: Marty Bucella, Dennis Daniel, David Espurvoa, Bill Frauhiger, Jonny Hawkins, Karl R. Kraft, Dik LaPine, Steve Phelps, Harley L. Schwadron, Goddard Sherman, Wendell W. Simons, Kevin Spear, Ed Sullivan, Andrew Toos, and M. Larry Zanco.

We would also like to thank Rebecca Price, Lisa Bergren, Laura Barker, and Carol Bartley of WaterBrook Press; Lenore Person and Elizabeth Gold of Guideposts Books; our agent, Sara Fortenberry; and Gerrie Bridge, FMC's administrative/editorial assistant, for their encouragement, persistence, and wise counsel.

God bless and smile on all who read this book.

—CAL AND ROSE SAMRA, editors

The Lord's Laughter

A merry heart doeth good like a medicine:
but a broken spirit drieth the bones.

—PROVERBS 17:22, KJV

40 years of ministry prepared Pastor Lou for his retirement years.

© Steve Phelps

Adam was very lonely in the Garden of Eden and told God he had to have someone besides God to talk to. God replied that He would give Adam a companion—a woman.

God said the woman will cook for Adam, wash his clothes, clean his home, bear his children, and take care of them.

The woman, God said, will always agree with every decision Adam makes and never argue with him. She will be full of love for him, and she will heal his wounds. She will never have a headache, and she will always be in good humor.

"What will a woman like this cost me?" Adam asked.

"An arm and a leg," God replied.

"What can I get for just a rib?" Adam asked.

—VIA BUD FRIMOTH, PORTLAND, OREGON

At the weekly Men in Motion luncheon at Central Baptist Church in Melbourne, Florida, the speaker was talking about the importance of forgiveness. He said, "The Lord has given me the command to forgive the wrongs of others, but He has not given me the ability to forget them."

From the back of the room, an older man interrupted the speaker: "Just wait a few years!"

—VIA PALMER STILES, MELBOURNE, FLORIDA

An atheist was sailing in Scotland when his boat was suddenly attacked by the Loch Ness monster. The monster flipped the sailboat in the air and opened its mouth to swallow him.

"Oh God, help me!" the man cried out. The monster froze and backed off. The man heard laughter and a deep voice from the sky declare, "I thought you didn't believe in Me!"

"Give me a break, God," the man replied. "Until a minute ago, I didn't believe in the Loch Ness Monster either."

—VIA LOIS H. WARD, PROSPECT, OHIO

Question: Can an atheist get insurance for acts of God?

—Rev. Karl R. Kraft, Mantua, New Jersey

The Billy Joe Wayne Ministries adopts a "hands-off" policy.

© Jonny Hawkins

Aaron Wymer, a minister for a Disciples of Christ church, told this story to a group of students at Florida Tech in Melbourne, Florida:

A man had been shipwrecked on a remote island in the Pacific, and was alone for 20 years. When a ship finally arrived, his rescuers were impressed with the three buildings he had built and asked him about them.

"Well," the man replied, "this is my house, and that building over there is my church. It's a wonderful church; and I hate to leave it."

"And what is the third building yonder?" a rescuer asked.
"Oh, that is the church I used to go to," the man replied.

—VIA PALMER STILES, MELBOURNE, FLORIDA

Twenty-five percent of the people think the pastor can walk on water; 25% think he doesn't know enough to come in out of the rain; and 50% are satisfied if church is on time and the sermon isn't too long.

—MSGR. JOSEPH P. DOOLEY,
MARTINS CREEK, PENNSYLVANIA

A doctor told a rich man that he would die in a couple of weeks. So the rich man called his three friends—the doctor, his preacher, and his lawyer—to his bedside. He said, "I am dying. My pastor has told me that I can't take it with me, but I think I've found a way. I have prepared three sealed envelopes, each containing $10,000 in cash. When I die, I want each of you to walk by the casket and drop in your envelope with the $10,000."

After the funeral, the three friends met together. The preacher said, "I've got a confession to make. We needed to repair the church organ, so I took $2,000 out of my envelope and used it for the organ. I only dropped $8,000 in my envelope."

The doctor confessed, "Well, I took $5,000 out for my new clinic and only dropped in $5,000."

The lawyer said, "My conscience is clear. I did just what our good friend Joe asked. I kept my envelope, picked up both of yours, and dropped in a check for the full amount of $30,000 made out to Joe."

—VIA REV. LARRY LEA ODOM-GROH, FIRST CHRISTIAN
CHURCH, CHILLICOTHE, MISSOURI

"All the members of my church tithe," a pastor told another pastor. "They all give 10% of what they ought to be giving."

—VIA BRUCE H. BURNSIDE, ROCKVILLE, MARYLAND

While officiating at a wedding ceremony at Skyline Christian Church in Idaho Falls, Idaho, minister Thomas Baird asked the groom, "Would you have these vows sealed with the gift of a ring?'

To Baird's astonishment, the groom reached into his pocket, took out a quarter, and flipped it into the air. Catching the quarter, he looked at it and then replied, "Yep."

The wedding ceremony then proceeded to its conclusion.

Albert O. Karlstrom of Champaign, Illinois, tells this chicken story:

"After a very delicious fried chicken dinner prepared by the Swedish Lutheran ladies at a missionary society conference held in our small church, the conversation moved from the dinner to other small talk. The speaker for the conference asked my mother, a pastor's wife: 'How many children do you have?'

"In the noise and commotion, my mother thought he asked, 'How many chickens do you have?' A normal question because most families in our small community had chickens in their backyards.

"My mother replied: 'I really don't know because my husband takes care of them. They stay penned up in the backyard, and he sees to it that meal scraps get out to them. Every now and then, one gets out, but that doesn't happen very often.'"

Preparing for a sermon, our pastor, John Koch, of Trinity Assembly of God in Crivitz, Wisconsin, got a great idea. On a

Saturday night, Pastor Koch with the help of a few congregation members, trashed the sanctuary with garbage, pop bottles and cans, old clothes and shoes, newspapers, and even socks hanging from the chandeliers. It was a mess!

Later that evening, a local police officer was checking the area and noticed the side door was unlocked. He walked in with his flashlight and, to his surprise, saw the mess. He got on his radio and told the dispatcher to call the pastor. The dispatcher called the youth pastor, Jay Fisher, and told him, "Your church has been broken into and ransacked."

"No, it's supposed to be that way," Pastor Jay replied, explaining that it was part of the object lesson for the next day's service.

The next day, people hesitated to even step foot into the sanctuary. Others ran wild. Pastor Koch started leading songs, then said, "Let's clean up this mess."

In five minutes, with the help of the entire congregation, the sanctuary was clean. Pastor Koch then began his sermon, and preached about getting the sin out of our lives so that we could be able to really come to God and worship Him.

—Mark and Susan Bradbury,
Wausaukee, Wisconsin

After a week of hot, steamy weather, speaking at the fashionable St. Andrew's Dune Church in Southhampton, England, guest minister Rev. William Henry Wagner told the congregation he would preach the shortest sermon in church history. This was Wagner's sermon: "If you think it's hot here, just wait."

—Via Paul Thigpen, Springfield, Missouri

© Dennis Daniel

Headline in December 1997 edition of the *Record*, publication of the Episcopal Diocese of Michigan:

"Bishop Richard Emrich dies,
returns to Michigan for eternity."

—*THE ANGLICAN DIGEST*

The Pope came to New York City and hailed a cab from the airport to St. Patrick's Church. The Pope was running late, and asked the cabby to speed it up. The cabby refused to go faster, so the Pope said, "Pull over and let me drive."

The Pope got behind the wheel, and very soon a police car pulled them over. The officer looked inside the car, and made a call to the police chief. He told the chief there was someone very important in the cab and they were speeding.

The chief told him to give him a ticket. The officer said, "But he's someone very important."

The chief said, "Well, who is it—the mayor? The governor? The President?"

"I don't know," the officer said, "but the Pope is driving him."

—VIA MRS. HARRIET ADAMS, MORTON, PENNSYLVANIA

It was a very hot day and the air conditioner at Christ Episcopal Church in Rockville, Maryland, had failed. The pastor, Rev. Linda Poindexter walked to the pulpit, looked out at the sweltering congregation, and gave this ten-word sermon: "Hot, isn't it? Hell's like that. Don't go there! Amen."

—VIA BRUCE H. BURNSIDE, ROCKVILLE, MARYLAND

HIGH-TECH PSALM

The Lord is my programmer. I shall not crash.

He installed his software on the hard disk of my heart;

All of His commands are user-friendly;

His directory guides me to the right choices for His name's sake.

Even though I scroll through the problems of life,

I will fear no bugs, for He is my backup;

His password protects me;

He prepares a menu before me in the presence of my enemies;

His help is only a stroke away.

Surely goodness and mercy will follow me all the days of my life,

And my file will be merged with His and saved forever.

—AUTHOR UNKNOWN, VIA GEORGE GOLDTRAP, ORMOND-BY-THE-SEA, FLORIDA

A committee is a gathering of important people who singly can do nothing, but together can decide that nothing can be done.

—Comedian Fred Allen

You know you are in the wrong church when...
- the church bulletin lists the senior pastor, the associate pastor, and the psycho-pastor.
- the choir wears black leather robes with studded collars.
- during the offering, you observe that all of the ushers are armed.

—via Rev. Karl R. Kraft, Mantua, New Jersey

"I sometimes think about the mysterious origin of life, the vastness of the universe, the complexity of the human brain and nervous system, the awesome beauty and diversity of nature, microscopic creatures and millions of living things beneath the sea, and all the laws that keep everything from crumbling into nothingness, and I say to myself, 'Arnold, maybe there's a God, but, hey, maybe there isn't.'"

© Ed Sullivan

ODE TO THE THIRD STANZA

I think that I shall never see

A resurrected stanza three:

The third, with oft the salient thought

Revealing why the hymn was wrought;

The third, which sometimes bares the soul

The hymnist wanted seen as whole;

The third, replaced by interlude

Through which we stand in somber mood;

"Let's sing the first, the second and last,"

The way we've done it in the past!

Hymns are sung by folk like me,

But only God sings stanza three!

—DAVID A. ROBB OF DALTON, GEORGIA, PASSED ON HIS THOUGHTS ON RECEIVING THE THIRD *STANZA*, AN OCCASIONAL PAPER OF THE HYMN SOCIETY IN THE UNITED STATES AND CANADA. © DAVID A. ROBB. REPRINTED WITH PERMISSION, AND WITH APOLOGIES TO JOYCE KILMER.

Annoyed by complaints from some parishioners that incense used during mass was choking them, the pastor of Our Lady of Mt. Carmel Church in Niles, Ohio, placed the following announcement in the church bulletin:

"Please Note: For our liturgical celebrations, a non-choking incense will be used."

—FR. JOHN TRIMBUR, OF ST. JOHN THE BAPTIST CATHOLIC CHURCH IN CAMPBELL, OHIO, PASSED ON THIS ITEM WITH THE COMMENT THAT HE HAD DOUBTS THAT THERE WAS ANY SUCH THING AS "NON-CHOKING INCENSE" ON THE MARKET. BUT ANOTHER READER, LINDA RADEN, WHO IS A SECRETARY IN A CATHOLIC DIOCESE, REPORTED THAT "WE USE A CHOKELESS INCENSE AT OUR CATHEDRAL IN GAYLORD, MICHIGAN."

Question: How many bass-baritones in a church choir does it take to change a light bulb?

Answer: Three: One to climb the ladder and do the job, and the other two to sit there and say, "Isn't that a little too high for you?"

—BRUCE H. BURNSIDE, ROCKVILLE, MARYLAND

An old hellfire and brimstone preacher was always preaching that the worst was coming—maybe tomorrow. One day he asked a member of his church, "What would you say if I told you that tomorrow all the world's rivers and creeks were going to dry up?"

"Well, the man replied, "I'd say, 'Go thou and do likewise!'"

—GEORGE GOLDTRAP, ORMOND-BY-THE-SEA, FLORIDA

ON "BLOVIATING"

Syndicated columnist James J. Kilpatrick, a well-known wordsmith, wrote a column about the art of overkill. "In our business, the writing business, sometimes we try too hard," Kilpatrick observed. "The novelist comes down with adjectivitis, the preacher succumbs to bloviation, and the newspaperman tries his hand at purple prose."

According to *Webster's World Dictionary*, the word "bloviation" does indeed exist. "To bloviate" is "to speak at some length bombastically or rhetorically."

METEOROLOGY

After listening to a political speech on the TV nightly news and then watching the telecast's weather report, Fred Sevier of Sun

City, Arizona, wondered how a meteorologist might report a political speech or some TV sermons. Possibly this way:

"Beginning light and breezy with some intermittent hot air. Quickly becoming very windy, with gusts up to 200 words a minute, and a jet-stream of verbosity, with thoughts going counterclockwise around the central issue. Then becoming stormy, with much thunder but little enlightening; finally leading to a whirlwind conclusion, but leaving listeners in a fog."

"If you wish to get back to me during the day, my fax number is 426-8433 and my e-mail is bixby@bus.com."

© Harley L. Schwadron

A pastor's wife called a veterinarian who makes house calls and told him her dog was very sick and wouldn't move. When the vet arrived, he found the dog on the floor with his feet in the air.

He examined the dog but there was no response. He reached into his satchel, pulled out a live cat, moved the cat over the dog several times, and then put the cat back in his bag.

"I'm sorry, ma'am, but your dog is dead," the vet said. "That will be $430."

"Four hundred thirty dollars! For what?" the woman exclaimed.

"The fee is $30 for the house call and $400 for the CAT scan," the vet replied.

—VIA HENRY DOUGHTY, S. WOODSTOCK, CONNECTICUT

When a pastor joined a local service club in his community, some of the members of his congregation made up the nametags for the group. They decided to play a practical joke on the pastor by labeling his occupation as "Hog Caller" on his nametag.

When the pastor saw his nametag, he commented: "They usually call me the 'Shepherd of the Sheep,' but I suppose our members know themselves better than I do."

—VIA REV. DENNIS R. FAKES, LINDSBORG, KANSAS

In a large Episcopal church in Virginia, the senior warden was addressing the congregation as he wrote on a blackboard: "MD, DD, LLD."

"Today," the warden said, "we welcome back our rector, who is returning from a sabbatical year during which he earned another college degree. For the information of you younger members, the letters on the blackboard stand for 'Mairzy doats and dozy doats and liddle lamzy divey.'"

—VIA BRUCE BURNSIDE, ROCKVILLE, MARYLAND

Atheism: a non-prophet organization.

—VIA REV. KARL R. KRAFT, MANTUA, NEW JERSEY

Deacongestion: too many deacons at a meeting.

—LOWELL J. GOERING, HILLSBORO, KANSAS

"The stock market's down again. We may set a new attendance record yet."

© Goddard Sherman

One of the tasks I had in our monastery was to go to the health-care center, after our infirm sisters had finished their breakfast, and bring the food cart back to the main kitchen. Before return-ing, I would load any remaining food and/or dirty dishes on the cart. One morning a sister, noticing me put an empty platter on the cart, felt obliged to apologize, explaining: "There's no coffee cake left."

I exclaimed with some indignation, "Coffee cake...? No, that was *stollen!*"

Astonished, she responded, "Oh really? That's too bad, because we ate it all!"

—SR. MARY E. PENROSE, OSB, ST. SCHOLASTICA
MONASTERY, DULUTH, MINNESOTA

After he moved from a church in Connecticut to become rector at St. Ambrose Episcopal Church in Boulder, Colorado, Fellowship of Merry Christians member Rev. John Elledge commented: "The people in my town in Connecticut seemed to think that one of the gifts of the Spirit is suspicion."

When the lights went out before the late service at St. Peter's Episcopal Church, Ladue, Missouri, one Sunday, the rector's sermon was still in the computer, unable to be printed because of the power outage. When informed of this, the congregation applauded.

—*THE ANGLICAN DIGEST*

When he entered the pulpit, one preacher realized that he had forgotten his sermon notes. He immediately apologized: "Since I forgot my sermon notes, I must rely on the Lord for this sermon. I promise to come better prepared next Sunday."

—REV. DENNIS R. FAKES, LINDSBORG, KANSAS

A man's house should be on the hilltop of cheerfulness and serenity, so high that no shadows rest upon it, and when the morning comes so early, and the evening tarries so late, that the days have twice as many golden hours as those of other men. Home should be the center of joy.

—HENRY WARD BEECHER

"Have you ever noticed that whenever the pastor leaves on vacation, he always gets a replacement who talks longer than he would?"

Bifocals Can Make Life More Fun After the Big 4-0

"I can't find the books on Divine Guidance."

© Jonny Hawkins

The following is excerpted from Forty Reasons Why Life Is More Fun After the Big 4-0 *by humorist/encourager Liz Curtis Higgs, a consulting editor for* The Joyful Noiseletter *who lives in Louisville, Kentucky. (Reprinted with permission of Thomas Nelson Publishers, Nashville, Tennessee. © 1997 Liz Curtis Higgs.)*

Reason 36 why life is more fun after the Big 4-0: *Bifocals let you look down your nose at everybody.*

The brochure at my optometrist's office made it all sound so simple: "If you're over 40 and are having trouble reading up close, you probably have a common and natural condition called *presbyopia.*" Sounds more like the fear of becoming a Presbyterian.

Maybe decreasing vision is a spiritual problem: "Now the eyes of Israel were dim with age, so that he could not see" *(Genesis 48:10, NKJV).* Yes, Israel, we understand. So sorry bifocals weren't invented yet. They might have been a big help to you. *Might* is the key word here.

On the day that bifocals showed up at my life's doorstep, my eye doctor, a pretty 30-something redhead with flawless skin and perfect vision, leaned over, patted my hand (making me feel 4 or 74, I'm not sure which) and said softly, "It's time, Liz."

I could feel the tears rising in my throat. Blinking and swallowing, I plastered my face with a big, brave smile. "Great!" I said, but didn't mean it.

"You'll learn to love bifocals," she said, and didn't mean that either.

It was awful.

I ordered the "Progressive Addition Lenses" (the kind without the line) which the brochure insisted would give me "a full range of uninterrupted vision, more like the natural vision of your youth!"

Gosh, can't they do better than *that?* By the time I was 21, my eyes tested at 20/350. I want the natural vision of a young woman who can see herself in the mirror from across the sink.

My friend Rita, 45, says with a sigh, "I'll yield to gray hair and a few extra pounds, but vanity hangs tough when it comes to giving up my contacts for a pair of bifocal specs."

My friend Deb, 47, was equally appalled. "I finally admitted I needed them when I couldn't read the hymnal when I held it in the usual position, and I couldn't fasten a brooch because I couldn't see the clasp. I've compensated by buying several pairs of 'vanity glasses,' to match my moods or outfits!"

Meanwhile, at my friend Bonnie's house, she and hubby are both wearing trifocals. When they sit and chat "our heads bob around like those little dogs on the dashboards of cars!"

"Love at first sight" takes on a whole new meaning after 40: Now I *love* when I can *see* something. Anything. I used to buy my grandmother those magnifying sheets for Christmas. Hope Santa can fit one in *my* stocking this year.

© Steve Phelps

But all shall be well
and all shall be well
and all manner of
things shall be well.

—Julian of Norwich

3

Tips to Help Pastors Buy a Used Car

"It'll be your own personal option... just imagine this baby with *stained-glass windows*."

© Ed Sullivan

The following tips come from humorist Rev. David R. Francoeur of Stuart, Florida, who has served several Episcopal churches in the South and is a consulting editor to The Joyful Noiseletter.

The Reverend Peter Nurplowe has completed a five-year study whose purpose was to develop some principles and techniques to help pastors buy a used car.

Reverend Nurplowe dressed up like a pastor—sometimes

wearing a priest's collar and sometimes wearing a suit and carrying a Bible—and visited car dealerships across his state with the presumed intent of purchasing a used car.

Nurplowe reported that "I 'negotiated' right up to the moment when the salesperson brought out the paperwork, and then, while feigning a search for the men's room, I quietly slipped away."

He discovered these principles:

- Wearing a clerical collar does not guarantee an automatic clergy discount. In fact, it may well increase the price.
- A warm, pastoral style does not thaw an ice-hard position on a car's price by a salesperson. In fact, the "smoother" one attempts to be, the less likely the salesperson will budge.
- The negotiation potential of car buying puts most clergy at a disadvantage since the process contains a high degree of conflict potential and clergy are traditionally more comfortable avoiding conflict.

Nurplowe reported that he discovered various techniques which were "helpful in creating a favorable negotiation at my end, and which I recommend that clergy use."

- Begin the negotiation with prayer. When you and the salesperson return from your review of available stock (or after the test drive), invite the salesperson to join you in prayer. This is sure to derail the salesperson's train of thought. It would be wise to fill the content of your prayer with direct references to both God's presence in your midst and His verifiable anger over the mistreatment of His children.

•Remind the salesperson that you have taken vows of
poverty.

When entering the actual negotiation phase, appear relaxed
and serene while the salesperson is praising the virtues of the
car and the reasonableness of the price. It is especially helpful if
you will keep an open Bible in your lap—open to one of many
passages which will provide divine guidance should the salesperson become unwilling to cooperate on the price.

•When negotiations break down, be prepared to share
your faith with the salesperson.

Here is an example of how Reverend Nurplowe used this
technique with a salesperson:

SALESPERSON: Pastor, I have gotten the price so low that
even Jesus Himself couldn't have done better. If I go back to
my sales manager again, he'll fire me. That would put me and
my wife and children out on the street.

PASTOR: I don't believe that God is going to let you and your
family starve. God wouldn't do that. God is a most gracious
and giving God. Just consider the price He expects me to pay
for this car!

•When the salesperson begins to waver in his resolve,
bring God directly and forcefully into the battle on your
side. It is here where the power of the "prophetic utter-
ance" can take hold. Example:

SALESPERSON: I'm sorry, pastor, I just can't do any better on
this price.

PASTOR: Forgive me. While you were speaking, I was whisked
away from this mortal sphere to a place of great glory. Everywhere there was a light brighter than we have seen in this world.

My eyes caught the silver strains of choirs of angels. Incense caressed my nostrils. On a throne of magnificence there presided the Lord God Almighty Himself, looking upon me with eyes of limitless compassion and beckoning me to come forward...

SALESPERSON: Yes!...Yes!...Go on!

PASTOR: God spoke to me!

SALESPERSON: Yes!...Yes!...What did He say?

PASTOR: He said: "Lower...the price must be lower."

Reverend Nurplowe concludes that he "has found the techniques outlined above contain the greatest possibility for success for the enthusiastic pastor, if they practice what they preach."

He recommended the following books as resources:

Wheeling and Dealing with Guilt and Shame by Tarnwell Clastover.

Christian Conversions at Auto Dealerships by Petular Vostenberry, Ph.D.

"Here you are, sir – a computer list of people whom you can fool some of the time."

A sure way for someone to lift himself up is by helping to lift someone else.

—BOOKER T. WASHINGTON

4

"The Carol Burnett of Christian Comedy"

"Mom. They're fighting over watching 'Touched by an Angel,' or a re-run of 'Highway to Heaven.'"

© Ed Sullivan

They call her "the Carol Burnett of Christian comedy." FMC member Kay Dekalb Smith comes on the stage wearing a brightly colored bathrobe and a wig with curlers, and carrying a plunger in one hand and the Bible in the other.

"My family always knows when dinner is ready because the smoke alarm goes off," she says, and her audience howls.

"My mother's house is so clean, you can eat off her floor. But you can eat off mine and get a full three-course meal!"

She wraps a vacuum cleaner hose around her body like a giant snake, and using a dust mop as if it were a guitar, she belts out satirical songs like "Lord, Change My Spouse," "I'm a Minister's Wife," "God Made a Mistake," and a song about balancing the checkbook.

She tells funny stories about chasing her two small daughters with a fly swatter, the trials of hormonal ups and downs, and hot flashes.

She does hilarious impressions of Shirley Temple and Alfalfa. Then she talks about Proverbs 31 and the love of Jesus.

This effervescent, forty-four-year-old, red-headed singer-comedienne, who lives in Brentwood, Tennessee, does about a hundred performances a year around the country, appearing at churches, conventions, universities, and other special events.

But, she says, "home and family are Number One. I really mean that the Lord is Number One, but I feel that if my family is not in order, my relationship with Him is always out of whack."

Her husband, Ed Smith, is business administrator at First Baptist Church in Franklin, Tennessee, which the family attends. They have two daughters, Allie, ten, and Evin, fourteen.

She says she stayed single until the age of twenty-eight, and after "investigating every male in Nashville," she finally prayed to the Lord to transfer the right man in. Shortly after, Ed Smith's bank relocated him from Kentucky to Nashville.

Kay says she was "raised in one of the few functional families that are left. My parents experienced the joy of the Lord daily. Our house was full of laughter. My parents didn't beat up on me—they laughed at me. I've tried to pass on that joy and laughter to my family and other people."

Her daughter Evin once told her: "Mom, if I ever lost you in the mall, I know how I'd find you. I'd just follow the laughter."

As Miss Alabama Teenager in 1972, Kay made national TV appearances in Billy Graham Crusades and later joined the cast of "I Hear America Singing" at Opryland USA.

She says she's "always felt the need to sing and to make people happy."

"There were five first-time decisions, eight re-dedications, and 46 'That was the best rendition of Elijah's ascent in a flaming chariot I've ever seen.' All things considered, I'd say it was a great spring retreat."

© Steve Phelps

BIBLIMERICKS

Lois Blanchard Eades of Dickson, Tennessee, writes "Biblimericks." Here are some she passed on to *The Joyful Noiseletter:*

> When Eve gave the apple to Adam,
> They did what Jehovah forbade 'em.
> As might be expected,

When they were detected,
He said, "Don't blame me; blame the Madame."

The confusion of language at Babel
Did not put a stop to the gabble;
For folks north and south
Still ran off at the mouth;
But it messed up a good game of Scrabble.

The Pharaoh encouraged his daughter
To bathe as a good princess oughter;
But he wasn't too glad
When she hollered, "Hey, Dad!
Just look what I found in the water!"

The animals entered with Noah;
When God shut and bolted the doah.
The dinosaur cried,
"My wife is outside!"
That's why dinosaurs are no moah.

Once Jezebel said to Elijah:
"I'll kill ya 'cause I can't abide ya."
It frightened the prophet,
But God said, "Come off it!
I know of a cave where I'll hide ya."

ONE-LINERS

There is nothing more miserable in the world than to arrive in Paradise and look like your passport photo.

—ERMA BOMBECK

The duty of a toastmaster is to be so dull that the succeeding speakers will appear brilliant by contrast.

—CLARENCE B. KELLAND

If no one ever took risks, Michelangelo would have painted the Sistine floor.

—NEIL SIMON

"I'm leaving the church and taking my favorite pew with me!"

I would rather try and cool down a fanatic than try and warm up a corpse.

—JOHN WESLEY

Walk a mile in his shoes before you criticize a man. Then, if he gets angry, you're a mile away and he's barefoot.

—AUTHOR UNKNOWN

October is one of the peculiarly dangerous months to speculate in stock. The others are July, January, September, April, November, May, March, June, December, August, and February.

—MARK TWAIN

Keep your face to the sun and the shadows will fall behind you.

—POLYNESIAN PROVERB

Out of the Mouths of God's Kids

A priest readying young candidates for confirmation informs them that the bishop will be coming to test them on how well they know their catechism.

The priest instructs them on everything from matrimony to purgatory.

On the appointed day, the bishop conducts an exam. "What's matrimony?" he asks Johnny.

"Matrimony's where the poor souls go to suffer until they're admitted to heaven," Johnny answered.

—COLUMNIST TOM RADEMACHER, *GRAND RAPIDS (MICHIGAN) PRESS*

Our daughter, Jennifer, eleven, has never been a patient person. Everything has to be done right now. When she was five, she saw her older brother baptized, so she wanted to be baptized.

We tried to explain that she needed to be old enough to understand the commitment she was making to Christ. A few nights later, we heard violent splashing noises and spluttering coming from the bathtub.

I called out, "Jennifer, what are you doing?"

She replied with a shout, "I told Jesus I loved Him and baptized myself!"

—LARRY J. CROCKER, MINISTER, MARBACH CHRISTIAN CHURCH, SAN ANTONIO, TEXAS

An old, well-worn family Bible caught the attention of a small boy. He thumbed through the pages, looking at the illustrations. He found an old leaf pressed in between two pages.

The boy shouted to his mother, "Look what I found, Mommy! Adam's suit!"

—WINSLOW FOX, M.D., ANN ARBOR, MICHIGAN

My four-year-old son and his sisters (ages eight and twelve) were having a discussion about the names of the books of the

New Testament. My older daughter called out, "Matthew, Mark, Luke, and John."

My son asked, "John Smith, who goes to our church?"

My older daughter replied, "No, I think it's John the Baptist."

My son asked, "Does he go to our church, too?"

"No, we're Methodist," my eight-year-old daughter answered.

—LANA CALVERY, GREENVILLE, TEXAS

After church, a small boy announced to his mother: "When I grow up, I want to be a pastor. It's an easy job!"

"Why do you say that?" his mother asked.

"Because you only have to read one book," the boy replied.

—VIA REV. ROBERT M. THOMPSON, CORINTH REFORMED
UNITED CHURCH OF CHRIST, HICKORY, NORTH CAROLINA

During children's time at worship at Claysburg (Pennsylvania) United Methodist Church, Rev. Barry Neal asked the children, "Why do people ring a bell?" He expected the children to answer, "So people will come to church."

A little boy, however, replied: "To start the fight."

Before a Christmas pageant at St. Joan of Arc Church in Phoenix, Arizona, a small boy portraying the innkeeper in Bethlehem was instructed to turn away Mary and Joseph from his inn. The boy, however, felt so badly for them that he said, "There's no room at the inn, but would you like to come in for a drink?"

—LAURIE LALKO, PHOENIX, ARIZONA

"I think we've got this 'breaking bread together' thing down pretty good!"

A young boy was walking down the street pushing a lawn mower. A priest who was out in his yard said, "Hi, son. Where are you going with the mower?" The boy said, "I'm trying to sell it. I want to buy a bicycle."

The priest said, "How much do you want for it? We may be able to use a mower around the yard here." The boy thought thirty dollars would buy him a bicycle, so he sold the mower to the priest for thirty dollars.

A couple of days later, the boy rode by the rectory on his new bike. The priest was out in the yard pulling on the cord, trying to start the lawn mower. The boy said, "Oh, Father, you have to cuss a little to get that mower started."

The priest replied, "I've been a priest twenty-five years, and I've forgotten how to cuss."

The boy said, "You keep on pulling that cord, and it'll come back to you!"

—MRS. ROBERT F. SIMS, EUSTIS, FLORIDA

After Bishop-emeritus Kenneth Povish of Lansing, Michigan, instituted at his parish a weekly litany of divine praises of God for the holiness of the saints, a young mother attended with her son, a third-grader. After church, the boy asked his mother: "What's a spouse?"

"A spouse is somebody's husband or wife," the mother replied. "Why do you ask?"

"What does 'most chaste spouse' mean?" the boy asked.

"That means St. Joseph was a good, pure, and holy husband," the mother answered. "What do you think 'most chaste spouse' means?"

Rather reluctantly, the boy finally replied, "Well, I think it means that all the women were after him, but Mary got him in the end."

—VIA HARRIET ADAMS, MORTON, PENNSYLVANIA

J. J. Jasper, DJ for American Family Radio Network, mentioned on the air that he and his girlfriend, Melanie, were going to "say our vows" and get married. A six-year-old girl listening with her mother exclaimed, "Hey, Mommy, they're gonna say their vows. I know mine, too—A, E, I, O, and U!"

Fr. Robert A. Barbato, OFM Cap, was working in the garden at Old Mission Santa Inés in Solvang, California, when one of his parishioners walked by with her little daughter. The little girl pointed at Barbato and said, "Look, Mommy—it's the God from Church!"

Her mother carefully explained, "That's not God, honey. That's one of His friends."

The girl looked at Barbato, who was wearing dirty gardening clothes, and replied, "God's not too picky, is He?"

Our church, All Saints Episcopal Church, Sharon Chapel, in Alexandria, Virginia, was holding its first Liturgy of the Light of the World contemporary service. Twelve parishioners had been asked to stand in front of the congregation, one by one, and read an encapsulation of a verse from Thessalonians that each had been given.

Eleven parishioners stood and read their verses. A long pause ensued while we waited for the twelfth. Then from the back of the church, we all heard loud whispers of "Go," "Go!" "Now!" "Go!"

Finally, a young girl nervously walked up to the front of the church. Her one-word reading: "Encouragement."

—KAREN SUE PECK, SPRINGFIELD, VIRGINIA

After a disastrous organ breakdown on Easter Sunday morning, our congregation quickly replaced it with a new instrument. A few days later, I seated my three-year-old daughter, Sally, on the new bench to let her hear some of the sounds it made.

Her interest wandered to the nameplate. "What does that say?" she asked.

I replied, "Rogers. That's its name."

She said, "What was the old organ's name?"

"Allen," I replied.

She said, "I don't like either of those names!"

So I asked, "What would you name this organ then?"

After a wrinkled forehead and pursed lips, she proclaimed, "Fred!"

—REV. PETER C. LEATHERSICH, FIRST PRESBYTERIAN
CHURCH, APOPKA, FLORIDA

"So, did you give cheerfully or tearfully?"

In the kindergarten Sunday school class at Life Community Church in Sunnyvale Texas, the teacher told the children that Jesus was just like any other baby. She said, "Mary fed Him, and rocked Him, and sang to Him, and bathed Him, and changed His diapers…"

Every little mouth dropped open when the teacher said, "...and changed His diapers." They all sat there speechless.

Finally, Bethany, my niece, told the teacher: "Don't you think that's kind of personal?"

—VIA JANET BEHNING, LAUGH YOUR SOCKS OFF
MINISTRIES, MESQUITE, TEXAS

After a storm, Leola R. Goit of Brookings, Oregon, took her son Gary, then three, for a walk along the beach of the Pacific Ocean. The road was covered with foam.

The boy pointed to the foam and asked, "How much soap did God put in the ocean, Mommy?"

"While working for a degree in New York, my wife taught fourth grade in a local Catholic elementary school. She wanted to counteract anti-Semitism, so one day she reminded the youngsters that Jesus, Mary, and all the apostles were Jews.

A little girl in the back row raised her hand, stood up, and said, "I know that Jesus was Jewish at the start, but when He died on the cross, He turned and became Catholic."

—JIM SOMERVILLE, SCHOLA CONTEMPLATIONIS,
PFAFFTOWN, NORTH CAROLINA

A minister preached about Jesus walking on the water one Sunday morning. After the service, a mother asked her small son some questions about the sermon to see if he had been paying attention.

"No big deal," the boy said. "God made water—God walked on the water."

—VIA BEATRICE BARNETT, FORT LAUDERDALE, FLORIDA

© Ed Sullivan

Pastor Fred Sapp of the Lutheran Church of the Holy Trinity in Kailua-Kona, Hawaii, called the children up front on a recent Sunday morning, and talked to them about Jesus the Shepherd. Because the children in Hawaii don't know much about sheep, Sapp told them about sheep and herding and then asked if anyone knew what a shepherd's crook was.

A small boy jumped up and said, "Yeah, it's the guy who steals the sheep."

—BILLIE DICKE, OCEAN VIEW, HAWAII

Archbishop Daniel M. Buechlein of Indianapolis received the following message on a birthday card from a little girl: "I hope you're fine because it is your birthday. It was an honor to have you bless and say the Mass for our new beautiful church. Your hat (miter) could be in style. Well, just think, if people would wear a Dr. Seuss hat, I'm sure they'd wear your hat."

—THE *CRITERION*, INDIANAPOLIS, INDIANA

Three-year-old Haylie Born, daughter of Dr. Eric and Julie Born of Parchment, Michigan, was playing in the basement of her home when she spotted several large jugs. Dr. Born had inherited the jugs of homemade wine from his grandfather, the late Dr. Grant Born, whose hobby was wine-making.

"What is that?" Haylie asked her mother, pointing at the jugs.

"That's Great-grandpa's wine," her mother replied. "He died and went to Heaven many years ago."

"Why didn't he take them with him?" Haylie asked.

During our church's Wednesday night activities a week before Halloween, six-year-old Michael came to me to show off the neat biblical costumes which the children had made for Halloween—tunics, headdresses, etc.

He was really proud of them, and with wide eyes he said: "Yeah, these are the kinds of clothes that the children wore when God was alive!"

—REV. WARREN J. KEATING, FIRST PRESBYTERIAN CHURCH, DERBY, KANSAS

I'm a Franciscan and usually wear my Franciscan habit. Last Halloween I was giving treats to quite a few small kids, all in costumes looking like witches, goblins, etc. One little fellow looked up at me and asked, "And who are *you* supposed to be?'"

—Fr. Ambrose German, OFM, St. George Church,
Hermann, Missouri

Visiting their grandmother's house, two young boys were saying their prayers at bedtime. The younger boy started loudly shouting his prayers: "God, please send me a Nintendo...and a new bike...!"

"Why are you shouting your prayers?" his older brother asked, "God isn't deaf."

"No, but Grandma almost is!" his little brother answered.

—via Thomas G. Bassett, Syracuse, New York

© Jonny Hawkins

A Sunday school teacher was teaching her class the Lord's Prayer. After a week of practice, she asked each child to stand and recite the Lord's Prayer individually.

A little boy said, "Lead us not into temptation, but deliver us some E-mail."

—VIA PATTY WOOTEN, SANTA CRUZ, CALIFORNIA

When my six-year-old granddaughter visited our small country church for the first time, she was awed by the communion service. Accepting the bread and then the wine, she whispered excitedly to me, "Do we get cheese, too?"

—MARIAN HOLBROOK, TRAPHILL, NORTH CAROLINA

When our three-year-old son came up with what sounded like, "Is God nuts?" we had to ask him to repeat the question. We wondered what awful worldly truth he might have discovered at his age. But he was in fact asking, "Is God in nuts?"

His sisters were cracking walnuts, and it seemed a wonderful discovery for him to test out the belief that "God is everywhere."

—DONNA OPAT, LINDSBORG, KANSAS, FROM *OVER THE BACKYARD FENCE*

During a Sunday school class of grade schoolers, I shared the information that Josiah had become king of his country when he was eight years old. I asked an eager eight-year-old lad, "Do you think you could be the king of a country?"

After a pause, he replied, "No, but I could be vice president."

Later, I asked the youngsters, "Do you know what *obedience* means?"

Without hesitation, one enthusiastic young lad declared,

"It's a school for dogs!"

—DICK MILLER, THE UNITED METHODIST CHURCH OF
WOOSTER, OHIO

A three-year-old boy was attending his infant sister's baptism at Hammond Avenue Presbyterian Church in Superior, Wisconsin. When the pastor, Rev. R. C. Reese spoke the words "...now in the presence of God...," the boy spoke up excitedly, "Did he say *presents?!*"

—BARBARA A. ZELL

"Of course it's a re-run! It's summer, isn't it?"

© Goddard Sherman

After Marge Squire's Sunday school class at Hunter Community United Methodist Church in Franklin, Ohio, one youngster, Tyler Smiddy, ran up to his mother and exclaimed: "Guess what? I'm psycho!"

"What do you mean?" his mother asked.

"I'm psycho," little Tyler replied. "I can see the future."

—VIA REV. R. VERNON BABCOCK, FRANKLIN, OHIO

Getting ready to go to church, Mrs. Gay Miller of Stillwater, Oklahoma, told her four-year-old boy to put on his shoes. She then discovered that he had put his right shoe on his left foot, and his left shoe on his right foot.

"You've got your shoes on the wrong feet." she said.

"They're the only feet I got," replied the boy.

—VIA DON COOPER, M.D., STILLWATER, OKLAHOMA

A few years ago, while teaching my morning confirmation class, I noticed the slowest, least interested pupil was watching me intently during the lesson. Suddenly, he raised his hand and asked the first question he had ever asked in the class.

I was wearing my clerical shirt with the collar tab, and the boy asked, "How do you get your head through that collar?"

All I could think of to say was, "You've heard of pin-headed preachers?" I pulled out the tab to show him.

—REV. GEORGE R. NAUMANN, LUTHERAN PASTOR, YORK, PENNSYLVANIA

On Wednesday nights, we have Pioneer Clubs, including story-telling for the children, at our church. My wife took the children into the church library, which has red velvet chairs. When eight-year-old Ryan sat down in one of them, he asked my wife, "Have you ever been in here before?" Then he added, "Of course you have—you're the pastoress."

—PASTOR BILL MAYHEW, FIRST BAPTIST CHURCH, BILLINGS, MONTANA

I am a pastoral associate at Nativity Parish in Akron, Ohio. One day, little Tim stopped by to chat, and I asked him if he prayed for me when he said the rosary with his family.

He replied, "I didn't even think of you." I then asked, "Will you remember me the next time you say your prayers?" Tim shrugged and said with a sigh, "I have so many people to pray for."

Then he asked, "Do you know Father Finnerty?" (Fr. Finnerty, who had celebrated the wedding of Tim's parents, had just died.) "Yes," I said, "how do you know him?" Tim responded enthusiastically: "Oh, I first met him when he was dead!"

—Sr. Susanne Gill, HM

In a children's sermon, Rev. Gerald Krum, pastor of St. John's Evangelical Lutheran Church in Lewistown, Pennsylvania, told the story of the time the young Jesus and his family went to Jerusalem, and when they started home, his family discovered that Jesus wasn't with them.

Krum asked the children where Jesus was, and they said he was in the Temple. When he asked what Jesus was doing there, there was a long silence until four-year-old Haley replied, "He was reading the bulletin."

Within an hour of Mother Teresa's death, the front door of a Missionaries of Charity convent in New York was inundated with roses, chrysanthemums, and other flowers left by people from the neighborhood. Eight-year-old Alex Santana said his bouquet was left with the message, "I hope you have a good time in heaven."

—DAVID BRIGGS, THE ASSOCIATED PRESS

When you tell a child that Washington never told a lie, make sure you make it clear that you're talking about the man and not the city.

—VIA CATHERINE HALL, PITTSBURGH, PENNSYLVANIA

Little children, let us not love with word or with tongue, but in deed and truth.

—1 JOHN 3:18, NASB

"Before they met Jesus, weren't the 12 disciples the Dirty Dozen?"

© Jonny Hawkins

Things That Spell Trouble at a Wedding

© Steve Phelps

Rev. Paul Lintern, a regular contributor to The Joyful Noiseletter *and the associate pastor of First English Lutheran Church in Mansfield, Ohio, offers the following warning signs at a wedding.*

After officiating (as in referee, as in umpire, as in field judge) at many weddings, I have discovered several signs that indicate that there might be some difficulties in the marriage, signs that may forecast troubled times ahead.

Take the word of this pastor for it. If you notice any of these circumstances at a wedding you attend or plan, beware:

- The processional song chosen is from a Metallica album.
- The mother of the bride asks whether the wedding will be over in time to get to bingo.
- The time of the wedding must remain flexible because the groom's parole hearing is set for that morning.
- The unity candle goes out.
- The couple chooses as its Scripture passage the story of Cain and Abel or of King David arranging the death of Uriah the Hittite in order to have the man's wife, Bathsheba.
- Three fathers arrive to usher the bride down the aisle.
- The ushers are reluctant to leave their automatic weapons at home.
- The bride considers the best man better.
- During the vow, the groom calls the bride by his former girlfriend's name.
- The couple argues over who will get custody of the unity candle.
- During a reflective time in the ceremony, the soloist sings about a brick house.
- Just before the vow, the groom asks, "Is this like, really official? Like, how easy is it to back out?
- The videographer's notebook has the address of "America's Funniest Home Videos."
- The bride's pager goes off, and she has to run to the office for "an important meeting."

- Two pews of pregnant women sob uncontrollably as the groom says, "I do."
- The caterer yells, "Can you hurry up the sermon, preacher? These croissants won't stay fresh all day."
- The couple fights over the day being ruined because one of them forgot to order a limousine.
- The recessional hymn is "Turn Back O Man, Forswear Thy Foolish Ways."
- The solo sung during the lighting of the unity candle is Frank Sinatra's "My Way."
- The bridesmaids' dresses have more chains than lace.
- The vow ends with "as long as we both feel like it."

"Yes or no, John. There's no plea bargaining here!"

At a wedding attended by FMC member Marvin Breshears of Yakima, Washington, the processional hymn for the seating of the mothers was printed in the wedding bulletin as "Come Undo Me" (instead of "Come Unto Me.")

"We wondered if you could take up a love offering for our wedding. You could call it the tithe that binds."

© Jonny Hawkins

FOR BETTER OR WOOF

Lois Blanchard Eades of Dickson, Tennessee, contributed this poem as a commentary on an article in the *Nashville Banner* about a man who was using his dog as a wedding attendant:

My friend endorsed Will Rogers; words profound:

"The more I see of humankind, the better

I like the canine kind," so altar-bound,

He ordered a tuxedo for his Setter.
"On second thought," he said, "omit the pants
For fear that they might turn a trifle soggy."
My friend was wise to circumvent this chance;
For such a deed would be no more than doggy.
Dog had his day. He middle-aisled it well,
For he'd been taught to heel. He took his place,
For he'd been taught to sit. Who could foretell
That he would lend such dignity and grace
To an occasion which was stranger than
Your average wedding? Dog was friend's best man.

"Best sermon on love I ever heard, Pastor."

A good marriage is the union of two forgivers.
—RUTH BELL GRAHAM

Bloopers That Gnash the Teeth

"You'll notice I'm getting some things off my chest in this week's bulletin."

© Ed Sullivan

From a church bulletin:

"The audience is asked to remain seated until the end of the recession."

—VIA PATTY WOOTEN, SANTA CRUZ, CALIFORNIA

From the bulletin of St. Francis of Assisi Church in Bradford, Pennsylvania:

"Father John _____ will be the homeliest each evening."

—VIA WILLIAM J. O'DONNELL

Headline in ad of Unity Church on the church page of the News Press *in Fort Myers, Florida:*

"Come Grown with Us"

—VIA CARL E. WAGNER JR., TOWSON, MARYLAND

From the bulletin of Covenant Moravian Church, York, Pennsylvania:

"Inquirer's class: Are you interested in learning more about the Moravian Church? Then your pooprtunity starts Sunday, March 8 at 9:15 A.M.!"

—VIA PASTOR DEAN JURGEN

From a pastor's column in a Berrien County (Michigan) church newsletter:

"The childbirth and superfluous activities carried on by Sunday Schools in the past make them seem superfluous to their alumni."

—VIA REV. ROBERT L. LIVINGSTON, BELCHERTOWN, MASSACHUSETTS

The Assembly of God Church of Bushnell, Florida, received a computerized sweepstakes notice announcing that "God, of Bushnell, Florida" was a finalist for the $11 million top prize.

"God, we've been searching for you," the letter from American Family Publishers said. "If you win, what an incredible fortune there would be for God! Could you imagine the looks you'd get from your neighbors? But don't just sit there, God."

Commented Pastor Bill Brack: "I always thought He lived here, but I didn't actually know. Now I do. He's got a P.O. Box here."

Following a lengthy and heated congregational meeting, the secretary presented the minutes for the pastor's review. The pastor reviewed them and asked the secretary to read her report of the motion to establish an executive committee.

Her record of the motion stated, "We need to establish an execution committee."

—Rev. Gerald R. O'Connor, Immanuel United
Church of Christ, Bartlett, Illinois

My first call to parish ministry was to a church in Michigan's Upper Peninsula. This congregation had a strong Finnish background. I wasn't prepared for the challenge of Finnish names.

I hadn't realized how much I was concentrating on pronouncing Finnish names until my first Christmas service. At the Christmas morning service, I turned to the congregation and announced our closing hymn: "Good Christian Finns Rejoice!" Needless to say, they did.

—Rev. Robert Fisher, St. Paul's and St. John's
Lutheran Churches, Ironwood, Michigan

Rev. James A. Gillespie of Charleroi, Pennsylvania, recalls that he was visiting an old bookstore in downtown Pittsburgh when he overheard a woman asking the store manager for "a Bible with an accordion in it."

Gillespie says he came to the rescue of the puzzled manager, whispering to him that what the woman really wanted was a Bible with a concordance.

© Harley L. Schwadron

A Catholic man has a heart attack and falls on a sidewalk of a city street. "Get me a priest!" the dying man tells a police officer coming to his aid.

The police officer asks the gathering crowd if there is a priest among them. No one comes forward.

"I need a priest, please!" the dying man cries out.

Finally, an elderly man in the crowd steps forward and says, "Officer, I'm not a priest or a Catholic, but for many years I lived next to a Catholic church, and every night I listened to the Catholic litany. Maybe I can be of some comfort to this poor man."

The old man kneels down next to the dying man and says solemnly:

"O-72, G-51, B-5, N-33, I-20..."

—VIA BUD FRIMOTH, PORTLAND, OREGON

Rev. Ken Grambo of Camrose, Alberta, who serves two Lutheran congregations in Alberta, was calling attention to various parts of the service printed in the Sunday bulletin. "Let us join now in confessing our sins, which are printed in the bulletin," he said.

FMC member Mark Kihn recently substituted for his pastor at his Lutheran church in Calgary, Alberta. At the end of the service, he gave a few announcements and then walked away from the pulpit. Then, realizing he had forgotten one announcement, he hurried back and said, "Oh, I'm sorry I almost forgot about the Alzheimer's workshop…"

The telephone number of the rectory of Whitesand Parish in Kamsack, Saskatchewan, is listed in the white pages of the telephone book as "Anglican Rectory." When the rector, Rev. Ian C. Payne, answered the phone recently, a telemarketing caller asked, "Is Mr. Anglican home, please?"

In the call to worship printed in the bulletin of First Presbyterian Church of Shadyside, Ohio, after the congregation had read the line, "God has not forgotten us," the lay liturgist was supposed to read the line, "Could a mother forget the child she has nurtured?" Instead, the liturgist read, "Could a mother forget the child she has neutered?"

In the front pew a woman who was about eight months

pregnant could not contain herself and laughed and laughed and laughed.

—REV. ALICE L. PHILLIPS

Our Presbyterian church once had an interim minister who, unnerved by the size of our congregation, made a couple of very funny bloopers during her sermons. She referred to Paul's letters to the "Philippines." And at Christmas she raised her arms to heaven and declared, "Today, Christ is bored."

—LORRAINE AHO, NOVATO, CALIFORNIA

Blooper in the intercessions for August 16, 1998, at St. Thomas the Apostle Church, Sheffield Lake, Ohio:

"We pray that the politicians will act in our best interests for the goof of the people."

—VIA FR. STEVE SHIELDS

"That's a nice thought, Sister Ida, but I'm not sure it's biblical to put a 'Coupon Good For $5.00 Off Your Next Tithe' in our newsletter."

© Bill Frauhiger

Jonathan Edwards (1703-58), the eminent American preacher and theologian, once remarked to Samuel Johnson, the English literary lion: "You are a philosopher, Dr. Johnson. I have tried, too, in my time to be a philosopher, but I don't know how. Cheerfulness was always breaking in."

8

On Giving Devotions

"I believe your father would like to add something."

© Bill Frauhiger

Quaker humorist Tom Mullen, former dean of the Earlham College School of Religion, has been a consulting editor to The Joyful Noiseletter *since its beginnings. An associate of the late Elton True-blood, Mullen is the author of* Laughing Out Loud and Other Religious Experiences. *The following excerpt from his book* Where Two or Three Are Gathered Someone Spills the Milk *is used by permission of Friends United Press. (© Tom Mullen.)*

In the life span of nearly every Christian, whatever his degree of backsliddenness, will come the inevitable invitation to give devotions. Public meeting or private gathering, secular event or sacred occasion, church service or horse show—the Law and the Prophets decree that someone must give devotions.

Public devotions fall into certain categories. There are "instant devotions," sometimes called "God will lead the way." Such devotional meditations will be characterized by no preparation whatsoever, as the leader will simply flip open a Bible and, as they say in the theater, "wing it." Unfortunately, the listeners to such presentations often "wing it" too, as their minds fly to distant psychological shores.

A second category can be identified as "ultra-traditional" or "the little old church in the wildwood" syndrome. This is perhaps the most widely used type of devotion and leans heavily on back copies of the *Upper Room,* the farther back the better.

Couched in the language of Zion, these devotionals sound the way devotions are supposed to sound, and the listeners will depart the meeting with peace of mind, knowing that holy language has been used even though they can't remember what was said.

Frequent devotion-givers often fall into a third category which is aptly described as the "TV dinner" variety. This means that the leader steals his material from somebody else's book and simply warms it up for public consumption.

Relying on a source unfamiliar to the laity, such as *The Pastor's Friend* or *999 Stories to Warm the Heart By,* the leader attempts to breathe life into dry bones by introducing the material with phrases such as "A funny thing happened to me on the way to the church." Such devotions as these are almost always harmless, thereby meeting the primary test of appropriateness for both sacred and secular occasions.

A popular kind of devotional in recent years has been the "avant-garde" meditation, sometimes called "nouveau blah." College teachers and preachers hoping for honorary doctorates exemplify this category. The key to this type is a dependence upon French existentialist writers, such as Camus and Sartre.

What these givers of devotions say is much less important than whether or not they pronounce French names properly. Avant-garde types utter such inclusive phrases as, "You are undoubtedly familiar with the helpful words of Descartes...," to which their audiences respond by smiling and nodding, even though most of them think the leader is referring to a Canadian hockey player he saw on TV the night before.

Another contemporary type is represented by the "liturgical litany boys." These persons always pass out stained mimeographed sheets of paper for reading and response. While the intention—to involve the audience—is a noble one, almost always these leaders pick out the best parts for themselves.

They usually read a long, sonorous part, to which everyone else is to reply, "Yea, verily." Sometimes the liturgy is written in the vernacular, however, and the expected response is changed to "You can say that again, Charlie..." —and he usually does.

A final category is the "Teutonic school" of devotions, characterized by totally incomprehensible content and numerous references to German theologians and their favorite phrases. The leader speaks of "Angst" and "Heilsgeschichte" and quotes Barth and Bonhoeffer as often as possible, usually with a certain tremolo in his voice. Such devotions are very helpful, as the audience feels profound without knowing why.

To whatever school we belong, however, we still share a

common dilemma. How do we worship Almighty God in Spirit and Truth? How, with authenticity, does the creature approach the Creator? Our gimmicks, our intelligence, our clever efforts to bring about "worship"—all are found wanting much of the time.

© Ed Sullivan

Sheer joy is God's and this demands companionship.

—THOMAS AQUINAS

9

Signs and Wonders

"It's a dogma-eat-dogma world."

© Jonny Hawkins

In Sioux Falls, South Dakota, they call FMC member Rev. Jeff Hayes "Pastor Pun." Hayes amuses and cheers up passersby with the daily puns and witticisms he puts up on the outdoor church sign of Faith Temple Church.

Hayes, associate pastor, now has a collection of over 500 sayings for church signs. Here are some of them:

"Church Ushers Always Pass the Buck."

"Ham It Up Here and You'll Do Some Bakin' There."

"The Heart of God Is Never in Need of a Bypass."

"The Great Physician Still Makes House Calls."

"If You Think You're Too Cool for God, You'll Warm Up."

"Zacchaeus Went Out on a Limb for Jesus."

"Our P.A. System Guarantees a Sound Sermon."

"Fellow Ship? We're All in This Boat Together."

"Old Preachers Never Die; Just Turn Them Out to Pastor."

"Author of the World's Best-Selling Book—Here This Sunday."

"Come On in and Tithe One on During the Offering."

"Old Deacons Never Die; They Continue to Make Motions."

"A Grounded Christian Life Is Electrifying."

"Sunday's Special—In by 11, Out by 12."

"On Pins and Needles? Jesus Will Cushion You."

"Getting Old? Jesus Can Put a New Wrinkle in Your Life."

"Spiritual Health and Fitness Club."

"Sorry but the Fruit of the Spirit Doesn't Include Sour Grapes."

"Wanted: Large Mouth Bass for Church Choir."

"Bank on It— God's Interest in You Never Changes."

"Happy Hour Now in Progress."

"The King of Hearts Enables One to Play with a Full Deck."

"Have You Hugged Your Pastor Today?"

"Trashed? God Can Recycle You."

"Confessions Heard Every Monday from Weekend Fishermen."

"The Pits of Life Can Sprout a Peach of a Person."

"We Welcome All Denominations—$1, $5, $10, $20, $50, $100."

"Soul Food Served at Every Service."

"If Life Is in Darkness, Turn On De Light."

"Thanksgiving: No Whining, Only Dining."

"Christmas: It's a Boy!"

"Christmas: A Stable Baby for All of the Fruitcakes and Nuts."

"No Gloom in the Tomb."

"Shepherds of the Flock Never Fleece Their Sheep."

"And God Rested on the Seventh Day and Mom Took Over."

"Don't Lose Your Peace of Mind by Giving Someone a Piece of Your Mind."

"Discouraged? Encourage!"

"God Can Always Peace Things Together."

"Hope Causes the Son to Rise in Our Mourning."

"The Message from the Pulpit Will Pull You from the Pit."

After reading the last of these church signs, Rev. Fredrick L. Haynes of Prince of Peace Lutheran Church of Russell County, adapted it as follows:

"The Message from This Pulpit Will Pull You from the Pit...Not Roast You over It."

Here are some other signs passed on to *The Joyful Noiseletter*:

Sign on the outside wall of a Maryland convent:

"Trespassers Will Be Prosecuted to the Fullest Extent of the Law."

—THE SISTERS OF MERCY

Sign seen in the parking lot of a church:

"Anyone Who Parks Here Preaches Next Sunday."

—VIA M. VILLALOVOS, PICO RIVERA, CALIFORNIA

Sign outside the First Baptist Church in Perry, Ohio:

"For a Special Treat, Try One of Our Sundays."

—BARBARA J. HERBEL, ENGLEWOOD, COLORADO

On a church sign in central Georgia:

"Patience Is a Virtue That Carries a Lot of Wait."

—VIA REV. WOODY McKAY JR.,
STONE MOUNTAIN, GEORGIA

Ad in the Ellsworth (Wisconsin) American:

"Village Dry Cleaners has relocated to 14 High Street, right next door to St. Joseph's Church. After March 1, cleanliness *is* next to godliness."

—ROBERT WAGNER, MILWAUKEE, WISCONSIN

© M. Larry Zanco

Sign in a Marshall, Michigan ice cream parlor: "Notice: If You Are Grouchy, Irritable, or Just Plain Mean, There Will Be a $10.00 Charge for Putting Up with You."

—VIA MATT SAMRA

Report of the
Search Committee

We have investigated a number of candidates of the ministry, but we regret to report that none seems suitable. Here are the comments on those we have considered so far:

Noah. Has 120 years of preaching experience, but not a single convert.

Moses. Stutters. Also loses his temper. Can be very violent.

Abraham. Goes to Egypt in hard times. Known to lie when in trouble.

David. Immoral. Might be considered for Minister of Music, if he had not fallen.

Solomon. A reputation for wisdom, but does not practice what he preaches.

Elijah. Inconsistent. Folds when under pressure. Retreats into caves.

Isaiah. Has unclean lips; admitted it in a worship service.

Jeremiah. Too emotional. Cries a lot. Alarmist. "Pain in the neck," some say.

Amos. No seminary training. Should stick to picking figs.

John the Baptist. Popular, but lacks tact and dresses like a hippie. (Considering his diet, he would not be happy at church suppers.)

Peter. Actually denied he knew Christ. Could not lead evangelism committee.

Paul. Preaches well, but contemptible appearance. Long sermons; people sleep.

Timothy. Has potential. Background questionable. Too young.

Jesus. Offends large segments of the audience when he preaches. Very controversial. He even offended the search committee.

Judas. Practical. Leadership abilities. Served on an executive committee. Good with money. Conservative spender. Cares for the poor. We were ready to make him our choice when he suddenly died. You never know about some people.

REPRINTED WITH PERMISSION OF *THE ANGLICAN DIGEST*

"Just where have you been for the last three days?"

IN THE BEGINNING…

In the beginning, God created heaven and earth. He was challenged immediately with a class-action suit for failure to file an environmental impact statement.

At last, He was granted a temporary permit for the project, but soon was handed a cease-and-desist order enjoining Him from creating on earth.

At the government hearing, God said, "Let there be light." The bureaucrats demanded to know how the light would be made. They asked if there would be thermal pollution, or strip mining.

God replied that the light would be created from a huge ball of fire. God was granted provisional permission to make light (1) if He would obtain a building permit, (2) if no smoke would result from the ball of fire, and (3) if He would keep the light on only half the time to conserve energy.

God agreed and said He would call the light "day" and the darkness "night."

Then God said, "Let the earth bring forth green herbs and many seeds." The EPA agreed, as long as native seed was used.

Then God said, "Let waters bring forth creeping creatures having life; and the fowl that may fly over the earth." Officials insisted that this would require approval from the Department of Game.

When God said He wanted to complete the project in six days, the officials informed Him it would take at least two hundred days to review the application and the environmental impact statement. Then there would be a public hearing followed by a twelve-month waiting period.

Then God created hell.

—FMC Member Steve Feldman of Jefferson City, Missouri, passed on this story by an unknown author.

Two bees met near a flowering bush. "How was your summer?" one bee asked.

"Too cold. Too much rain. Not enough flowers or pollen," the second bee replied.

"There's a bar mitzvah going on down the block. Lots of flowers and fruit. Why don't you go down there?" the first bee suggested.

"Thanks!" the second bee said, and flew away.

Later, the two bees encountered each other again. "How was the bar mitzvah?" asked the first bee.

"Wonderful!" said the other bee.

"But what's that on your head?" the first bee asked.

"A yarmulke," the second bee answered. "I didn't want them to think I was a WASP."

—VIA SARA A. FORTENBERRY, HERMITAGE, TENNESSEE

And God said. . .

$$\frac{mv^2}{r} = \frac{Z e^2}{r^2}$$

$$mvr = \frac{nh}{2\pi},$$

$$r = \frac{r^2 h^2}{(2\pi)^2 m Z e^2}$$

$$E = \frac{1}{2} mv^2 - Z \frac{e^2}{r}$$

$$E = \frac{2\pi m Z^2 e^4}{n^2 h^2} = Ry$$

. . . and there was Light.

— *Passed on by Patricia P. Karnosh*
New Philadelphia, OH

How to Counsel
the Counselors

"Sir, would you come with me? It has come to our attention you have been peeking when the pastor says, "With every head bowed, every eye closed…"

© Steve Phelps

The Joyful Noiseletter *consulting editor Stan Toler of Bethany, Oklahoma, is a longtime Nazarene pastor, humorist, and speaker who is associated with John Maxwell's INJOY Ministries. The following sampling is from his book* Minister's Little Instruction Book *(reprinted with permission of Toler and Honor Books. © Stan Toler).*

Here's some advice for pastors and lay leaders:

• Never go to the restroom with your lavaliere mic on!

- Never drive the church bus!
- Never handle the church money!
- Never go into business with members of your church.
- Raise your voice occasionally when you preach. There's nothing worse than a monotone.
- Never use an illustration about your family without permission.
- Use an illustration or humor every five minutes in your message.
- Let the congregation laugh at your mistakes publicly...they will anyhow!
- Don't use your preaching voice in everyday conversations.
- Keep breath mints in your suit pocket.
- Return your phone calls promptly!
- If you must counsel, counsel the opposite sex with the office door open.
- Reverse the divorce rate; marry only people who will accept premarital counseling.
- A church committee is the only life form with 12 stomachs and no brain.
- Growl all day and you'll feel dog-tired at night.
- Most people commit suicide with a fork rather than with a gun.
- Always go last in line.
- Exercise 15 minutes a day 5 times per week.
- Put cartoons in your church board reports. It'll lighten up the place.
- At age 20, we worry about what others think of us. At 40,

we don't care what they think of us. At 60, we discover they haven't been thinking of us at all. (Mike Duduit)

- When you must choose between a late night in the office or going home...go home!

© Dik LaPine

Signs of the Last Days

You know your days as pastor are numbered when...

- You're asked to be the donkey in the annual Christmas play.
- Without asking, your secretary photocopies and sends out your resume to 200 out-of-state churches.
- You find the visiting preacher's name on your mailbox.
- Shut-ins do not answer the doorbell when you come to visit.
- Your mother and spouse move their membership letters to another church.

- Church members refer to you in the past tense.
- The pulpit committee who hired you starts wearing sack-cloth.
- You come to church on Monday morning and find the locks have been changed.
- Your church splits, and the only thing the two groups can agree on is that neither group wants you as a pastor.

—VIA REV. KARL KRAFT, MANTUA, NEW JERSEY

NOT TOO COLD AND NOT TOO HOT

Pastor Fred Anson of Gloria Dei Lutheran Church in Toledo, Ohio, knows from experience that the water in the baptismal font can be too cold or too hot.

At his former church, during the rite of baptism, he reached into the baptismal font and discovered that the water was ice-cold. When he placed the water on the baby's head, the baby, he said, "let out a yell that would have raised Lazarus from the tomb."

When he came to Gloria Dei Lutheran Church, he made sure to ask the usher to put warm water in the baptismal font. The usher followed instructions and put the lid on the font.

When the time came to baptize a baby during the worship service, the parents and sponsors were standing around the font. When Pastor Anson removed the lid, a cloud of steam rose from the baptismal font.

"I will never forget the look on the mother's face," says Anson. "I motioned for the usher and whispered to him to bring some cold water and put it into the font. The baptism then proceeded.

After the service, I told the mother, 'My intention was to baptize your baby, not parboil it.'"

Rev. Ronald J. Mohnickey, TOR, of the Holy Spirit Monastery at the Franciscan University of Steubenville, Ohio, celebrated mass at a nearby church one hot summer morning. After the liturgy, a woman greeted him with a broad smile and said, "I am so happy when you celebrate mass here!" Before Fr. Mohnickey could respond, she added, "When you come here, they always turn on the air conditioning because you sweat so much!"

IN PRAISE OF A SUCCESSFUL PREACHER

From London, FMC member Bob White sends along this "Poem in Praise of a Successful Preacher," from the publication of St. Andrew's and St. Michael's Parishes (Church of England):

> We gave him twenty minutes
> He finished up in ten.
> Oh, there's a prince of speakers
> And a servant unto men!
> His diction wasn't very much;
> He hemmed and hawed a bit.
> Still he spoke a lot of sense
> And after that he quit.
> At first we sat quite paralyzed,
> Then cheered and cheered again.
> We gave him twenty minutes,
> And he finished up in ten.

Some ministers would make good martyrs; they are so dry they would burn well.

—CHARLES HADDON SPURGEON

One of the things Christ promised us was trouble. "In the world ye shall have tribulation," He said. But we must never forget that He added: "But be of good cheer"...or in other words, "Cheer up...I have overcome the world."

—PETER MARSHALL

"Chaplain Bill, I've been thinking. We've got to do something to get our prison church to go beyond its walls in 1999."

© Dik LaPine

"The Gospel Is Fun-Loving"

© Dik LaPine

FOSTERING THE FUN FACTOR

Not long after writing the following joyful article, Rev. Warren J. Keating, pastor of First Presbyterian Church in Derby, Kansas, surprised his congregation and his friends by announcing that he was dying after a six-year battle with multiple myeloma, a form of bone-marrow cancer. Keating said he was blessed to live into his sixth year when the prognosis was only two and a half years. "Through the bad times, I've been able to celebrate a lot more of the good stuff," said Keating. He said he celebrated life endlessly. He rejoiced when he saw a beautiful sunset. He was forever calling friends and telling them jokes. Keating went to the Lord a few months later. His friend Rev. Bob Henley of Eastminister Presbyterian Church in Wichita commented: "Through all kinds of circumstances, Warren tapped into a source of joy in his relationship with God through Christ. He just exuded joy. That is much deeper than happiness." This article is reprinted by permission from the June 1998 Net Results. *All rights reserved.* Net Results *is a monthly journal of "New Ideas in Church Vitality" published in Lubbock, Texas.*

The "fun factor" remains a seldom noted but hugely influential quality. Every pastor and congregation benefit from encouraging its highest possible level. The fun factor increases fellowship, simplifies complex decision making, and increases the church's magnetic attraction power for new attenders.

In our church the fun factor started on my second Sunday. A member had remonstrated me, "Lots of people don't like you wandering around all over the chancel area when you preach. You should stay in the pulpit like our other ministers have."

I decided to have some fun with that comment. As I introduced my sermon the following Sunday, I pulled out from behind the pulpit a huge plastic ball and chain. "Look what someone has put up here." I said. "I sure won't be able to move around with this tied to my ankle, will I? Guess I'll just have to free myself from this ball and chain."

Everyone laughed.

Instead of calling a meeting to discuss the pros and cons of pastors moving around the chancel when they preach, I made a joke of it. People laughed it off and forgot the whole thing. (I still wander around the chancel, but no one seems to care anymore.) That illustrates the power of the fun factor.

How to define the fun factor? It's joy! You see it on people's faces when they come to worship. You hear it in the excited conversational chatter when folks come in the door. When the fun factor is high, people connect with each other more easily, are more likely to express genuine concern, and more often exhibit joy.

One of the many reasons that children exert a positive influence on the quality of congregational life is their fun-loving nature. Notice what happens to adults during the children's time in worship. Children's fun-loving nature improves adults' attitudes and thereby increases their receptivity to spiritual insights.

Surely this expresses part of what Jesus meant when he said we need to have a childlike nature to experience the kingdom of God.

Humor and jokes do not equal Christian joy. Laughter is not Christian joy. But adults who take themselves less seriously seem far more likely to experience Christian joy.

A high level of fun factor allows me to use "Pop Rocks" in a sermon and get everyone to try some (Pop Rocks colored candy "explodes" in your mouth).

What crackling and popping more than 200 people make as they chew Pop Rocks at the same time! Laughter brings down defenses and lets people learn more readily.

We planned a Wednesday night dinner that featured chicken as the main course. The fellowship committee wanted everyone to come. During announcement time in worship, a group came up front dressed in crazy chef outfits. They played the "chicken" music and taught everyone the silly chicken dance. That can happen only in a church with a high level of fun factor.

Our puppet ministry promotes the fun factor (I have had a conversation with the puppets as part of my sermon). I have preached from a lawn chair. I had Santa Claus come and worship with us Christmas Eve.

I belong to the Fellowship of Merry Christians, which publishes *The Joyful Noiseletter*. We constantly share jokes and humorous stories with one another.

Because I wear fun ties, people give me ties such as "Looney Tunes" and "Popeye." I even have a tie that depicts Santa Claus fishing. On Father's Day I encouraged all the men to wear their wildest ties. We let the kids judge which one was the best.

Not every pastor wants to wear those kinds of ties. But every pastor, if he or she lightens up a bit, can experience the resulting mission and ministry benefits.

Leaders make or break the fun factor that helps to increase church health and growth. You've known sticks-in-the-mud, haven't you? You've known true-blue Presbyterians who have this motto engraved on their hearts—"decently and in order" (or that equivalent in other denominations). It's a great motto, but it's not the gospel. The gospel is fun-loving.

A picture of a laughing Jesus, entitled *The Risen Christ by the Sea*, hangs on my office wall. That picture has set the tone for my ministry. It's the first thing people see when they come into my office. Their comment usually is "Wow, I never knew that Jesus laughed. But I guess He did, didn't He? He probably had fun."

I believe we're on earth to delight each other, make each other laugh, and to infuse one another with His joy. Why not? What've we got better to do?

—BURT ROSENBERG, MESSIANIC JEWISH COMEDIAN, SILVER SPRING, MARYLAND

"All work and no play – brother, did you blow it!"

Hymn Game

"O.K! Let's really sing out on Psalm 119 – just the first and last verses."

© Wendell W. Simons

C. Justin Clements, director of the Office of Stewardship and Development, in the Catholic Diocese of Evansville, Indiana, went through one of his parish hymnals and put together the following "Hymn Game," assigning hymns to various professions and people.

"All Good Gifts"—The Lobbyist's Hymn

"All Shall Be Well"—The Hospital Administrator's Hymn

"All That We Have"—The Taxpayers' Hymn

"Change Our Hearts"—The Heart Surgeon's Hymn

"Come to Me, O Weary Traveler"—The Motel 6 Hymn

"Come to Set Us Free"—The Bail Bondsman's Hymn

"Comfort My People"—The Masseuse's Hymn

"Create a Clean Heart"—The Angioplasty Hymn

"Eye Has Not Seen"—The Optometrist's Hymn

"How Firm a Foundation"—The Contractor's Hymn

"How Great Thou Art"—The Weight Watcher's Hymn

"How Lovely Is Your Dwelling Place"—The Interior Decorator's Hymn

"I Saw Water Flowing"—The Plumber's Hymn

"I Want to Call You"—The Long-Distance Telephone Company Hymn

"Lord, You Give the Great Commission"—The Salesperson's Hymn

"Out of Darkness"—The Electrician's Hymn

"Shall We Gather at the River"—The Fisherman's Hymn

"Somebody's Knockin' at Your Door"—The Jehovah's Witnesses' Hymn

"We Shall Rise Again"—The Baker's Hymn

"What Star Is This?"—The Astronomer's Hymn

"Walk in the Reign"—Gene Kelly's Hymn

"All Are Welcome"—The Motel Manager's Hymn

"All That Is Hidden"—The Magician's Hymn

"Behold the Wood"—The Carpenter's Hymn

"Come Away to the Skies"—The NASA Hymn

"Come to the Water"—The Lifeguard's Hymn

"Come to the House"—The Realtor's Hymn

"For the Healing"—The HMO Accountant's Hymn

"Gather Us Together"—The Board Chairman's Hymn

"Guide My Feet"—The DUI Driver's Hymn

Before mass on Memorial Day weekend, the organist was play-ing songs with a patriotic theme. The church was very quiet. While the organist was playing "The Battle Hymn of the Republic," the small voice of an elderly woman near the front of the church was heard softly singing the lyrics.

When the organist played "God Bless America," the elderly woman began singing out with all of her heart, and kept on as if it didn't matter what anyone would think. I thought to myself—now there is someone who is truly moved by the Spirit and is full of joy!

—ANN RUESCH, ST. VINCENT DEPAUL PARISH,
WISCONSIN RAPIDS, WISCONSIN

"Thank you for that message on the Apoca-lypse, pastor. Now, let's all stand and sing, 'We'll Understand It Better Bye And Bye.'"

© Dennis Daniel

PRAYER OF A MELLOWING NUN

The Joyful Noiseletter *consulting editor Barbara Shlemon Ryan of Brea, California, invited readers to reflect on this whimsical prayer of an anonymous seventeenth-century nun:*

"Lord, Thou knowest better than I know myself that I am growing older and will someday be old. Keep me from the fatal habit of thinking I must say something on every subject and on every occasion. Release me from craving to straighten out everybody's affairs. Make me thoughtful but not moody; helpful but not bossy. With my vast store of wisdom it seems a pity not to use it all, but Thou knowest that I want a few friends at the end.

"Keep my mind free from the recital of endless details; give me wings to get to the point. Seal my lips on my aches and pains. They are increasing and love of rehearsing them is becoming sweeter as the years go by.

"I dare not ask for grace enough to enjoy the tales of others' pains, but help me to endure them with patience. I dare not ask for an improved memory, but for a growing humility and a lessening cocksureness when my memory seems to clash with the memories of others.

"Teach me the glorious lesson that occasionally I may be mistaken.

"Keep me reasonably sweet; I do not want to be a saint. Some of them are so hard to live with—but a sour old person is one of the crowning works of the devil. Give me the ability to see good things in unexpected places and talents in unexpected people. And, give me, O Lord, the grace to tell them so."

"Meet Howard Meely... perpetual sermon illustration."

Happy the eyes that see what you see.

—LUKE 10:23, TJB

"I Heard an Angel's Voice"

"It's okay if he has this thing for geese, but if he wants to land in a pond, I'm outta here."

© Ed Sullivan

FMC member Chuck Terrill is minister of Haverhill Christian Church in Augusta, Kansas. This story is from his book Hope and Hilarity: Positive Stories of Faith, Family, and Fun, *illustrated by Bryan Clark. (Morris Publishing. © 1996 Chuck Terrill. Reprinted with permission.)*

I was young and hadn't been a minister very long. It seemed like I was meeting resistance every step of the way in the small rural church that had called me to serve. It was my first church, and I was certain that the leaders were against me.

I resolved to prove my merit. I would be deep, theological, and aloof to their negativism. After all, I *had* been to Bible College. I would show those Midwestern septuagenarians that I had what it takes!

So I labored long and hard over my books. My sermons were punctuated profusely with words like *soteriology* and *pneumatology*. They collectively scratched their heads, and I wondered why I had not as yet gained their admiration and respect.

Furthermore, I resolved that my eight semester hours of Greek language study would not remain unused. I regaled the church with a variety of tense, voice, and mood. I honed my skills in etymology and lexicography. They did not respond.

I was about to give up the exposition of Greek as futile. But then, at a Wednesday Night Bible Study, a small breakthrough occurred. It was as if an angel of God had finally spoken and gotten through to the biggest blockhead of the bunch.

The lesson that evening was about love. It was a simple verse, really.

"This is the message you have heard from the beginning; we should love one another" (1 John 3:11, NIV).

I knew that there was a wealth of information lurking under the surface. So I carefully exposited the word *love* while completely exasperating the people.

I correctly informed the group that there are three different Greek words for "love." I listed and explained *phileo, agape,* and *eros.* I had them look up scriptures that used *agape* and *phileo.* Then came the crucial moment of truth. Could they give me concrete applications of the three terms? So I asked them.

"Who would give me an example of one of these three kinds of love?"

Nobody answered. They just sat there and stared at me. It was one of those awkward moments I had come to expect.

"Who can give me an example of one of these kinds of love?" I asked again.

It was then that the breakthrough occurred. My own little daughter was raising her hand! My heart felt so proud. This little four-and-a-half-year-old girl was about to put all of the people present to shame. She had been listening and could give an example of *agape, phileo,* or *eros.*

"Sarah," I asked smugly, "can you give us an example of one of these three types of love?"

She vigorously nodded. Confident.

"Sometimes," she blurted, "my Mommy takes a shower with my Daddy!"

I nearly died. My face went red. I glanced at my wife, who had covered her face with her hands. And then it happened.

One of the septuagenarians slapped his hand down on the table and let out a guffaw. He was laughing so hard that I doubt he even heard me confess that I had long since repented of showering with my wife.

But the others heard me, and their once shocked expressions were transformed into ones of unrestrained hilarity. Little Sarah, who had started it all, rocked back and forth in her chair and clapped her hands with glee!

I knew that I had lost them. The lesson was over! I did manage to gain enough composure to say a closing prayer, interrupted by an occasional, restrained snicker. Then I waited, shamefaced, for the group to leave.

They didn't leave though. They stayed. They talked. They laughed some more. I couldn't believe it. I didn't understand it. My wife and daughter were the center of attention.

Then Mr. Septuagenarian walked over and put his arm around me. He laughed again, and said, "I been tellin' everybody that you was human. They didn't believe me. Now that the truth is out, just relax. You don't have to impress us. Everybody here loves you. Just be yourself."

He patted me on the back and went over to rib my wife some more.

That's when the angel voice got through to the biggest blockhead of the bunch. Me.

"Everybody here loves you. Just be yourself."

My own little girl had probably given a better definition of the term *love* than even I could have imagined. And the weary congregation gave a wonderful application of the term.

Together, Sarah and that congregation had opened the door for a lifetime of loving, authentic ministry. I was so very relieved.

Converted, I swallowed my pride, walked over, and entered a lifetime of genuine ministry and laughter.

May the sun always shine on your windowpane.
May a rainbow be certain to follow each rain.
May the hand of a friend always be near you.
May God fill your heart with gladness to cheer you.

—OLD IRISH BLESSING

"I got the idea at my barber's."

© Goddard Sherman

Invasion of the Cucumbers

© Steve Phelps

*FMC member Rev. James L. Snyder is a minister with the Christian
and Missionary Alliance, currently serving the First Alliance
Church in Ocala, Florida. He writes a weekly humor column for
local newspapers. This article is reprinted with permission.*

The first congregation my wife and I served was small and the
stipend was in proportion. The dear people made up for the
small salary by sharing with us from their gardens. God faith-
fully provided for all our needs, sometimes with a healthy sense
of humor.

One Sunday while shaking hands with people as they were leaving the service, one lady asked, "Pastor, do you and your family like cucumbers?"

"Yes, we sure do," I answered. This was my first mistake. Her broad smile evoked another, "We really do like cucumbers."

I thought I was being friendly and did not anticipate just what was going to happen during the next few weeks.

Monday morning this lady was at the parsonage bright and early with several bushels of cucumbers, extremely pleased she could contribute to our well-being. By Saturday, my wife transformed the cucumbers into several quarts of pickles and relish.

The parsonage was connected to the church and little did we know the smell of pickles invaded the church. (By then we were accustomed to the smell and did not notice.)

"You folks really like pickles," one man said after the service.

"Yes sir, we do," I said with an innocent smile. My second mistake.

That next week, each day brought someone to our door with bushels of cucumbers. Even old Bill, a bachelor in the congregation who did not even have a garden, brought two bushels of cucumbers. He stopped at a roadside stand and bought them, "for my minister and his family," he told us.

That week my wife did everything she could think of with cucumbers. Cucumber sandwiches, cucumber salads, cucumber soup, bread and butter pickles, dill pickles, and relish. Her chief culinary creation was strawberry and cucumber pie (minus the strawberries.) Please don't ask me for the recipes.

They appeared faster than we could process them. One

night, under the sanctuary of darkness, I buried four bushels of cucumbers in a corner of the garden. Another mistake! The seeds sprouted and in a few weeks cucumbers took over a significant section of our garden.

When packing to move to Ocala, we discovered some boxes unpacked for several years. In one box were four quarts of pickle relish, the last of the cucumbers.

There was one benefit from all those pickles. No matter how pooped we were, eating all those pickles preserved our pucker power.

So, remember, when you find yourself in a pickle, it may just be God's provision for you, so relish it.

© Jonny Hawkins

PRESCRIPTION FOR THE BLUES

When Lutheran Pastor Denny J. Brake of Raleigh, North Carolina, gets up in the morning and "negative thoughts are buzzing in my head," he says he starts singing the first verse of Beethoven's "Ode to Joy." And the singing of the old hymn quickly scatters negative thoughts and moods.

The music for the hymn was written by Beethoven in the mid-1700s. Henry Van Dyke put words to it in the late 1800s and titled it "Joyful, Joyful, We Adore Thee."

> Joyful, joyful, we adore Thee, God of glory, Lord of love!
> Hearts unfold like flow'rs before thee, opening to the sun
>   above.
> Melt the clouds of sin and sadness, drive the dark of doubt
>   away;
> Giver of immortal gladness, fill us with the light of day.
>
> All Thy works with joy surround Thee, earth and heav'n
>   reflect Thy rays,
> Stars and angels sing around Thee, center of unbroken
>   praise.
> Field and forest, vale and mountain, flowery meadow, flash-
>   ing sea,
> Chanting bird and flowing fountain call us to rejoice in Thee.
>
> Thou art giving and forgiving, ever blessing, ever blest,
> Wellspring of the joy of living, ocean depth of happy rest!
> Thou our Father, Christ our Brother, all who live in love are
>   Thine;
> Teach us how to love each other, lift us to the Joy divine.

"No, Henry. 'The Feeding of the Five Thousand'
is not another one of the pastor's fish stories."

"Dr. Russell's Bible Diet"

© Harley L. Schwadron

In his forward to Dr. Rex Russell's best-selling book *What the Bible Says About Healthy Living* (Regal Books), Joe S. McIlhaney, M.D., writes: "Rex Russell is one of the funniest people I know. He has used his good humor, his medical expertise, and his knowledge of Scripture to help us learn what can enable us to have good health."

To improve your physical health and lift your spirits, Dr. Russell recommends that you add to your diet many of the natural foods which the folks in the Old and New Testament ate, while eating sparingly those foods which they ate sparingly or avoided.

He also recommends doing what those biblical folks did—an occasional short fast.

This advice comes from a physician who interned at the Mayo Clinic, currently is a radiologist on the staff at Sparks Regional Medical Center in Fort Smith, Arkansas, and is a member of the First Baptist Church in Fort Smith and a member of FMC.

So how did a Southern Baptist, Mayo Clinic-trained radiologist come to study and recommend what might be called "Dr. Russell's Bible Diet"?

As a young man, Russell had been a strapping football player on the Oklahoma State University team. In later years, he became diabetic. He also was suffering from chronic abscesses, arthritis, swelling in his legs, and deterioration of his arteries, eyesight, and kidneys.

"Because I'm a doctor, I searched for medical answers with many physicians," he says, "but only experienced continued illness and confusion.

"One evening in desperation I pulled a Bible off the shelf. I happened to come across Psalm 139:14, where the psalmist praises God because 'I am fearfully and wonderfully made.' I said: 'If we are so wonderfully made, why am I so sick? God, why didn't You give us a way to be healthy?"

He received this answer: "Rex, have your really read my Instruction Book?"

Searching the Bible, he discovered not only spiritual laws related to health, but also dietary and physical principles which he began to apply. After four years, this dramatic change in lifestyle resulted in the recovery of his health.

Although he still is dependent on insulin, he has not had an abscess or symptom of arthritis in 20 years. He now has 20/20 vision. His overall health has improved in every respect, he says.

Although he's not a vegetarian, Dr. Russell believes "most people in the United States would benefit from decreased consumption of meats."

The folks in the Bible, he says, ate meat sparingly, and considered meat "a celebration food," eaten only for special occasions, such as the return of a prodigal.

Living in the middle of catfish country, Dr. Russell also recommends that people avoid catfish.

In a chapter titled "Mom was right: Eat your fruits and veggies," Dr. Russell recommends a diet with plenty of fresh fruits and vegetables, grains, seeds, and beans—basically, the kind of natural diet that those Mediterranean folks were eating in biblical times and are, more or less, eating today.

Eat some garlic, too. If your spouse doesn't like it, tell him/her that medical research has shown that garlic lowers bad cholesterol levels significantly, lowers high blood pressure, and protects people from infections, according to Dr. Russell.

Another prominent biblical food, olive oil, has been shown by medical studies to have a beneficial effect on health, especially in preventing hardening of the arteries.

"The lifestyles of the young Hebrew, Daniel, and his friends provide great examples of the healthful qualities of vegetables and of eating according to God's law," Dr. Russell observes.

Carried into Babylonian captivity, Daniel and his friends were selected to serve the king in the palace. However, Daniel declined to eat the luxurious foods of the palace and received permission to eat only vegetables, lentils, and water.

"At the end of ten days, Daniel and his friends looked healthier and better nourished than any of the young men who ate the royal food (Daniel 1:15, 20)," says Russell.

Down through the centuries, periodic fasting and periodic abstinence from animal products also have been recommended by the Eastern Orthodox Church, the Catholic Church, various monastic traditions, and Protestant groups like the Seventh-Day Adventists. But many of the clergy and lay people of all denominations have not always taken these admonitions seriously, even during Lent.

Dr. Russell recommends three principles which he believes will improve a person's health. "They are not a cure-all," he says, "but I believe they will help all."

- Eat the foods God created for you.
- As much as possible, eat foods as they were created, before they are changed into nutrient-deficient or toxic products.
- Avoid food addictions. Don't let any food or drink become your god.

Dr. Russell has three other suggestions to improve one's health:

- Exercise regularly. "The Bible says: 'By the sweat of your brow you will eat your food.' (Genesis 3:19). Because most of us no longer toil in the fields for our food, physical exercise should be substituted. It is my belief that we need enough exercise to work up a sweat six days a week."
- Don't forget to smile. "Both the giver and the receiver of a smile benefit through the release of prostaglandins. These substances help balance the hormonal functions of the body."
- Everything in moderation (so said the apostle Paul).

"You're letting your refrigerator lead you into temptation."

© Goddard Sherman

"No, Matilda, the Bible doesn't mention how many calories there were in a serving of manna."

© Bill Frauhiger

And whenever you fast, do not put on a gloomy face as the hypocrites do.

—MATTHEW 6:16, NASB

Moving Testimony
of a Youth Pastor

"...for further precedent, may I refer to the case of
Faith Church versus Youth Pastor Kelly."

© Dik LaPine

Humorist Randy Fishell, a former youth and university pastor, is
associate editor of Guide. *This story is adapted from his book* Hair
Today, Gone Tomorrow *(© 1996 Review and Herald Publishing*
Association) and is used by permission.

Since our marriage began, Diana and I have had many moving
experiences. I'm sure we have moved more times than the cursor on my computer screen. If we live in one town for over a
year, we begin showing signs of *residophobia*—fear of staying in
one place too long.

Not that we have *wanted* to move so often. But it is uncanny how an empty bank account causes one to consider taking up serious employment.

We spend the weeks prior to a move gathering cardboard containers for packing. Rummaging through every dumpster in town carries with it the potential for misunderstanding, but you can't allow this to become a concern. You think of nothing but securing approximately one million boxes before the moving truck arrives.

In the matter of box gathering, I pass on a cognitive technique that will help you maintain a positive outlook: View the process as a treasure hunt. You and your spouse will become involved in exchanges like this one on a regular basis:

"My love, guess what I found at Safeway today!"

"I can hardly wait to hear, my sweetest!"

"A large-size Charmin and two banana boxes, complete with handholds!"

"Can it be true? Yes, it must be—even now I smell the scent of rotting fruitskins on your hands! Yet, my love, your joy is only a shadow of my own, for today I discovered something exceedingly wonderful behind 'Nutty' Bolton's Hardware Store: a double-wall air-conditioner box, with the bubble wrap *still in it!*"

Next comes filling these containers with your household goods. I consider myself a master of the Garage Tool Toss 'n' Stuff technique. I throw everything within the sound of my voice into a box, then mash it down with a few well-placed stomps for final closure.

We made our first cross-country move when I accepted a

position as a youth pastor in Seattle. For a couple of years we'd been living in an old house in Michigan, out in the "sticks."

As the moving van disappeared down the road, we strolled out and squeezed into our overstuffed, filled-to-the-gills automobile.

Beneath the front seat lay two prone, partially tranquilized felines. Add to them a dog, a pregnant wife, and me—the captain of this unstately ship—and you can guess that we felt somewhat less comfortable than a millipede with bunions.

When we hit Chicago, after torrential rains, the road on which we were traveling had become as congested as a pollen-filled nasal passage.

When our air conditioner conked out, we stopped at a service station, where a smiling mechanic brought us the glad tidings: "I can't fix this thing." It was getting close to 100 degrees outside.

In North Dakota, our tailpipe chose to separate from us, and our car suddenly emulated the sound of a fighter jet.

We eventually made it to Seattle. The first night in our new apartment, I longed to be cradled by our Therapeutic pillow-top mattress. Someday my dream would come true—when the moving van arrived.

Frankly, I would be satisfied with just one more move in my lifetime. I could move to a land that is fairer than day where, I believe, a place awaits me that I'll never need or want to leave. "In my Father's house are many rooms; if it were not so, I would have told you. I am going there to prepare a place for you. And...I will come back and take you to be with me that you also may be where I am" (John 14:2-3, NIV).

I'm eager to make that move. How 'bout you?

Let your hope keep you joyful, be patient in your troubles, and pray at all times.

—ROMANS 12:12, TEV

© Dik LaPine

A Young Pastor's First Hospital Call

"It's been this way ever since the Lord confirmed that He was calling me to a ministry of counseling adolescents!"

© Bill Frauhiger

The Joyful Noiseletter *consulting editor Cy Eberhart, a United Church of Christ chaplain who lives in Salem, Oregon, tours the country portraying the great American humorist Will Rogers in a performance packed with Rogers's funny observations on politicians and preachers. This story is reprinted with permission from Eberhart's book* Burnt Offerings—Parables for 20th Century Christians *(© Cy Eberhart).*

A new member in the ranks of the ordained got a nervous stomach whenever he thought of making a hospital call. In seminary he had sparred with spiritual comforting by way of approved textbooks. But now he was inside the ropes and expected to take on the real thing.

The closest he'd ever come to experiencing pain was a penicillin shot; and in the art of binding up wounds it was Band-Aids, iodine, and a kiss to make it well.

Nevertheless, there was a command burning inside him: "As you did it to one of the least of these my brethren, you did it to me." And his professor in Pastoral Care 256, Section B, had told him of the unspeakable joys in being God's vessel.

So, being a man of faith, he swallowed hard and advised his flock that in their moments of pain and loneliness, God's help was as near as the phone. He put his prayer book at the ready and waited for his moment of truth.

One evening, parishioner Johanson drove down the street and made an unexpected exit through the windshield, landing in the hospital's emergency room. His life was intact, but several bones needed realignment.

Hearing of the accident, the young pastor grabbed his prayer book and, en route to the hospital, dress rehearsed several comforting thoughts designed for such occasions. He came through the rehearsal as a tower of spiritual strength and a conveyor of great compassion. It was opening night, and he was ready.

Now his seminary books had neither pictures nor sound tracks, so what he was to see was a first for him. There stretched out with guy wires and pulleys, like a repair man in a machine shop, was Johanson. Tubes, needles, and gadgets protruded conspicuously from all over his body. His face was the color of sunset patterned with a black embroidery.

From the opening curtain it was stage fright. The pastor's mouth dried out; instead of his comforting thoughts he remembered he should be home preparing Sunday's sermon. His spirit fled. His body would have gone, too, except Mrs. Johanson was there watching.

A strange power held his tongue. He felt his pounding heart, the perspiration on his head, and his stomach shifting into reverse. Then the patient rolled his eyes, opened his mouth, and groaned something awful.

The symbol of God's presence cried, "Amen!" and fled.

Late the next morning, he stumbled out of bed and went to the kitchen to tell his wife he was leaving the ministry. But before he could open his mouth, she told him that Mrs. Johanson had called and said how his visit had helped them greatly. They had gained composure through his quiet, sensitive mood and found strength for the night through his silent prayer.

Moral: Being an amateur is not always a handicap.

AN ANGEL LIFTED HER DEPRESSION

A number of years ago (before I was a member of FMC!), I was hospitalized for severe depression. One morning, while sitting on the edge of my bed and spilling buckets of tears, a lady came and sat next to me. Not knowing that I was a Christian, she held my hand and related the following to me:

"The world was never sadder than on Good Friday when Christ was crucified, but just three days later, the world was never brighter than when Christ rose from the grave. Whatever your problem is today, it will seem a lot less worrisome to you if you can just wait three days."

This lady was not a nurse, and when I inquired about her later, no one seemed to know who she may have been. (My guardian angel perhaps?) I have clung to this thought for twelve years, and it has pulled me through many a trying time.

—EDITH CLOUD, JEFFERSONVILLE, PENNSYLVANIA

"Welcome to Fantasy Island, Youth Pastor Dave! Your fantasy of living your life without any teenager, parent, or senior pastor has been arranged."

© Dik LaPine

I was sick, and you visited Me.

MATTHEW 25:36, NASB

"Let my people go, or you will have to walk like that the rest of your life."

© Wendell W. Simons

When I have tripped up and fallen, doing serious damage to my joy and peace, I say, Lord, today I have made a fool of myself. I have said and done what I ought not to have done, but I believe Christ can save me, even me, and I will rest in Him still.

—CHARLES H. SPURGEON

The Sports Section

"There's nothing wrong with church attendance that getting Michael Jordan's endorsement wouldn't cure."

© Andrew Toos

In an ecumenical gesture, the Prime Minister of Israel challenged the Pope to a friendly game of golf. Not a golfer, the Pope called in a cardinal and asked him if he knew of a cardinal who could represent him in the game.

The cardinal said he knew of no cardinal who plays golf well, but "there is a famous American golfer who is a Catholic by the name of Jack Nicklaus. We can make him a cardinal, and he can play the Prime Minister of Israel as your personal representative."

Nicklaus agreed to play and was appointed a cardinal. After the match, Nicklaus telephoned the Pope and said, "Your Holiness, I have some good and some bad news. The good news is that I played the best golf in my life. My drives were long and true, and my putting was splendid."

"What's the bad news?" the Pope asked.

"I lost to Rabbi Woods by three strokes," Nicklaus replied.

—VIA REV. KARL R. KRAFT, MANTUA, NEW JERSEY

"Do you get the feeling that we're going to get out early today?"

Pete and Joe were the best of friends, and shared a lifelong love for baseball, from Little League to college. Pete was a pitcher and Joe was a catcher. As they grew older, they went together to many baseball games.

In their senior years, they often speculated as to whether there was baseball in heaven. They agreed that whoever passed away first would find a way to contact the other one and let him know if there really was baseball in the hereafter.

Joe passed away first. Years passed, and Pete never heard the answer to the question. Finally, one night at bedtime, he heard a voice say: "Pete, it's true! There really is baseball in heaven!"

"Joe, is that really you?" Pete asked.

"Sure it's me, and I want to tell you how great it is up here." Joe said. "I have seen Walter Johnson strike out Ty Cobb. And once I saw Babe Ruth hit a home run off Cy Young. I even got to catch Dizzy Dean in a game one time."

"That's wonderful to hear, Joe," said Pete.

"Yeah," said Joe. "I saw tomorrow's lineup card, and you're scheduled to pitch."

—VIA PAT AND AL SMITH,
FALLS CHURCH, VIRGINIA

Eau Claire Evangelical Faith Church was the first church on record that went through a church split over allegiances to pro football teams.

Shortly before he died, former Chicago Cubs and White Sox broadcaster Jack Brickhouse was asked to sum up all the years of watching bad baseball. Brickhouse replied: "If every bad game I watched reduced the time I spent in purgatory, I would spend no time there at all."

—Columnist John Shaughnessy, *Indianapolis Star*, via Dick Hassing

Dizzy Dean, the great St. Louis Cardinals' pitcher, was a country boy who sometimes mangled the English language. When he became a baseball announcer, a critic accused him of wrecking the syntax of students.

"Sin tax?" Dean replied. "What will those fellers in Washington think of next?"

After Cardinal John O'Connor wrote a column in *Catholic New York* criticizing major league baseball teams for playing on Good Friday, the *New York Post* carried a front-page story under the headline, "Sermon on the Mound."

BASEBALL IN OLDEN TIMES

> Eve stole first and Adam second,
> St. Peter umpired the game.
> Goliath was struck out by David,
> And a base hit made on Abel by Cain.
> Rebecca went to the well with a pitcher,

And Ruth in the field won fame.

The Prodigal son made a long home run,

And brother Noah gave out checks for rain.

—VIA JAMES A. GILLESPIE, CHARLEROI, PENNSYLVANIA

Mike Bimler of St. Louis was trying to help his small son, Aaron, with his baseball swing.

"That's okay, Dad," the boy said. "I'll strike out on my own!"

Boxing legend Muhammad Ali was quoted by *People* magazine as describing his Parkinson's disease as a "blessing." Explained Ali, 55: "I always liked to chase the girls. Parkinson's stops all that. Now I might have a chance to go to heaven."

"I trust your hearts are keenly focused on what the Lord has to say to us this evening, and not on the Lions' stinking loss to the Bears this afternoon on that lousy holding penalty call by the refs with 1:15 to go in the game!"

© Jonny Hawkins

Asked what coach George Karl told his team at halftime when the Sonics were trailing Vancouver 65-56, Seattle's Vin Baker replied: "Listen, I'm a minister's son. I don't repeat those kinds of things."

SUPER BOWL SUNDAY RITE IV

The following special Super Bowl Sunday liturgy was revised by Rev. Ernie Davis of St. Michael's Episcopal Church in Independence, Missouri:

I. Prior to the entrance hymn, the clergy will toss a coin. The winner may elect to be the homilist or presider. The loser may elect to defend the altar or ambo.

II. The Entrance Hymn: "Pass it on."

III. Rubrics:

A. The presider or homilist may be awarded three points for correctly announcing the Super Bowl Sunday alternate title: The (Quarterback) Conversion of St. Paul.

B. Any acolyte found in illegal motion will be assessed a five-yard penalty.

C. The reader may fake a handoff to the deacon and read the gospel, provided that changes in audible signals are clearly given.

D. A sermon in excess of 18 minutes will be regarded as "delay of the game," and the homilist will lose possession of the ambo.

E. The offering plates or baskets may be lateraled and gate receipts collected during halftime.

F. A Eucharistic prayer said in less than three minutes is penalized as "rushing." Use of a mumbled or off-key tone will be counted as a fumble. Possession of the altar will be awarded to the team in physical control.

G. The peace may be passed, only one of which may be a "Hail Mary." Abuse Prevention Guidelines must be observed.

H. Ineligible communicants (receivers) will forfeit their grace.

I. Ushers may blitz either the homilist or the presider only during announcements.

IV. The Lessons:

Exodus 14:22—Israelites make quarterback sneak across the Red Sea.

Ephesians 6:14-17—Dressing the players in the proper equipment.

Matthew 28:16-20—Jesus sends out the Eleven.

V. Choir Anthem: "Drop-kick me Jesus through the Goal Posts of Life."

VI. The Sermon: "Hallelujah!" or "Go Chiefs!" (Name of your favorite team may be substituted.)

VII. Memorial Acclamation: "Christ was back; Christ is back; Christ come way back."

From what we get, we can make a living; what we give, however, makes a life.

—ARTHUR ASHE

"This is madness, Frank. The Super Bowl is history."

© Ed Sullivan

Headline on the sports page of the *Detroit News* after Mark McGwire hit his record-breaking sixty-second home run:

"McGwire Is Spiritual."

The article by Lynn Henning noted that McGwire is a loving, hugging Christian and that he several times commented before the sixty-second home run: "When and if it happens, it is up to the Man upstairs." McGwire also talked about visiting Babe Ruth and Roger Maris in the afterlife.

During his exciting competition with Mark McGwire for the home run leadership, Chicago Cubs slugger Sammy Sosa was asked by a reporter who his hero is. Sosa answered: "God."

The Dominican Republic native captured the hearts of Americans with his warmth, smile, humor, and humility. In his home, a Spanish-language Bible is by a bed. In the Dominican Republic, they call Sammy Sosa "Sammy Claus" because of his charity and generosity.

But he won't talk about his many acts of charity. "I don't want to get a big head," he says. "I was raised religious, and I'm scared what would happen to me if I did that."

Growing Down

"Why do we need to be baptized in front of
the church when we can do it right here?"

© Kevin Spear

*The following story is from FMC member Dr. Paul R. Welter, a
counselor and father of four in Kearney, Nebraska.*

For the last fifteen years, I have been trying to put to work the
command of Jesus, "Unless you change and become like little
children, you will never enter the kingdom of heaven"
(Matthew 18:3, NIV). My awkward feeling tells me I have only
grown down to early adolescence so far.

In 1982, I began teaching "Learning from Children" at the University of Nebraska at Kearney. It is the only college class I know of with this title. It is always filled, and it attracts child-like adults who have a sense of wonder and who love children. Some are quiet, most are spirited, and a few are outrageous.

Two of the latter made the last day of class an unforgettable experience. I knew something was in the air. It was five minutes before class and not a student was in the room. Exactly five minutes later the class trooped in single file. All were in costume and carrying a balloon. Some were clowns, some were little children, and we had farmers, a fireman, and other occupations and life stages represented.

Two people did not arrive until a half-hour later. Terry is an elementary school counselor, and Mary Ann is a teacher in an alternative school for at-risk teens.

They were on their way to class from another city when they saw a woman walking along the highway. Her gait was a bit unsteady, and these veteran teacher-counselors sensed something was wrong. They went back and picked her up.

They soon discovered she was on medication, had left a psychiatric hospital without checking out, and had no idea where she was going. She became suspicious and said, "You're going to put me back in that hospital. Let me out!"

So they let her out, but were afraid she might walk into traffic. They went downtown to find the police station.

Mary Ann was gorgeously dressed as Scarlett O'Hara. She had a hat with a wagon-wheel-size brim and a luxurious blue dress with a full white-trimmed skirt. Terry had rented a man-size diaper with a bib top. He had a pink bonnet with strings that tied under his chin and a mustache that peeked out between the strings. A huge pacifier hung on a rope around his neck.

They stopped on Main Street and asked two elderly women for the location of the police department. The women spontaneously took each other's hands and started running. They finally found the police department, and two officers interviewed them. Terry said, "We're concerned about a lady who is acting rather strangely."

The officers' faces revealed what they were thinking. One of them asked for Terry's driver's license. Terry said, "Just a minute; it's in my diaper."

The officer said, "I cannot look at you and write this report at the same time." Nevertheless, they said they would go check on the woman.

By the time Mary Ann and Terry finished telling their story, we were all laughing so much we were crying.

Laughter is of great spiritual value because it self-distances us, especially when we laugh at ourselves. When we laugh, our eyes are taken off ourselves.

Viktor Frankl said that if one has a cataract, he cannot see others clearly because he sees a part of himself first. Laughter removes the cataract of "self-spectating," and allows us to become self-transcendent. Self-distancing is the first step in learning to love.

ROY ROGERS'S TOP TEN

Shortly before Roy Rogers, the King of the Cowboys, went to the Eternally Happy Trails, David E. Welsh, senior minister at Central Christian Church in Ocala, Florida, wrote this column in his church newsletter.

Do kids play cowboys anymore? To my knowledge, my kids never have. I guess kids of the nineties consider it old-fashioned.

But I grew up in the age of the Western. In those movies, you always knew who the bad guys were. And you always knew your heroes would be victorious.

Roy Rogers had his own group of fans called the "Roy Rogers Riders' Club." There were 10 rules you had to follow to be a member in good standing.

Many kids today would find them pretty lame. But as a former kid, Western fan, and now a Christian minister, I still find them relevant:

1. Be neat and clean.
2. Be courteous and polite.
3. Always obey your parents.
4. Protect the weak and helpless.
5. Be brave but never take chances.
6. Study hard and learn all you can.
7. Be kind to animals and care for them.
8. Eat all your food and never waste any.
9. Love God and go to Sunday School regularly.
10. Always respect our flag and country.

Happy trails, pardners...till we meet again!

"Slingshot, squirt pistol, tacks, rubber bands, spit wads, frog... Yep! I'd say we're well-equipped for Sunday School!"

© Bill Frauhiger

Today may the sun shine on your world;
may the rain fall on your garden;
may the clouds pass over your troubles;
may the stars twinkle on your life;
may the moon brighten your journey;
and may tonight bring you a better tomorrow.

—IRISH BLESSING, VIA REV. JOHN H. FAHEY,
WASHINGTON, WEST VIRGINIA

You Might Be in a Country Church If...

David Espurvoa © Ron Birk

Lutheran Pastor Ron Birk, a consulting editor for *The Joyful Noiseletter,* has authored several very funny books, including *St. Murphy's Commandments.* Birk is also a Texas goat rancher whose ancestors all were involved in farming or ranching.

He has "great love and respect for country people, their churches, and their humor." So he put together a book called *You*

Might Be in a Country Church If..., a collection of observations about country church life illustrated with cartoons by David Espurvoa (© 1998 by Ron Birk; LangMarc Publishing, San Antonio, TX; reprinted with permission). Here are some samplings.

You might be in a country church if...
- The doors are never locked.
- The Call to Worship is "Y'all come on in!"
- People grumble about Noah letting coyotes on the Ark.
- The preacher says, "I'd like to ask Bubba to help take up the offering—and five guys stand up.
- The rest room is outside.
- Opening day of deer hunting season is recognized as an official church holiday.
- A member requests to be buried in his four-wheel-drive truck because "I ain't never been in a hole it couldn't get me out of."
- In the annual Stewardship Drive there is at least one pledge of "two calves."
- Never in its entire hundred-year history has one of its pastors had to buy any meat or vegetables.
- When it rains, everybody's smiling.
- Prayers regarding the weather are a standard part of every worship service.
- A singing group is known as "The O.K. Chorale."
- The church directory doesn't have last names.
- The pastor wears boots.
- Four generations of one family sit together in worship every Sunday.

- The only time people lock their cars in the parking lot is during the summer—and then only so their neighbors can't leave them a bag of squash.
- There is no such thing as a "secret" sin.
- Baptism is referred to as "branding."
- There is a special fund-raiser for a new septic tank.
- Finding and returning lost sheep is not just a parable.
- You miss worship one Sunday morning and by two o'clock that afternoon you have had a dozen phone calls inquiring about your health.
- High notes on the organ set dogs in the parking lot to howling.
- People wonder when Jesus fed the 5,000 whether the two fish were bass or catfish.
- People think "Rapture" is what happens when you lift something too heavy.
- The cemetery is in such barren ground that people are buried with a sack of fertilizer to help them rise on Judgment Day.
- It's not heaven, but you can see heaven from there.
- The final words of the benediction are, "Y'all come on back now, ya hear!"

In His great wisdom, God at Creation designed the human body so that we can't pat our own backs or kick ourselves.

—AUTHOR UNKNOWN, VIA CATHERINE HALL,
PITTSBURGH, PENNSYLVANIA

"According to my horoscope, this is a good week to preach against false doctrines."

The Appliance Man Ringeth

"Ever since we were expelled from the garden I've had this worry about paying something called 'bills.'"

© Ed Sullivan

Ann Weeks is a nurse family therapist in Louisville, Kentucky. The foregoing story is reprinted with permission from her book She Laughs and the World Laughs with Her *(© Ann Weeks).*

One of the many challenges that I was confronted with after my first husband's death was people calling and asking to speak to him. Paul was an attorney, and calls from clients and others unaware of his death continued for weeks.

One evening a couple of months after Paul's death, the phone rang. "Hello, Kleine-Kracht's residence," I stated.

"May I speak to Paul Kleine-Kracht?" a man asked.

I caught my breath and said, "I'm sorry, Paul is deceased. I'm his wife. May I help you?"

Without any comment about what I'd just said, the caller jumped right in with, "I'm John Jones with the Appliance Warranty Center. I'm calling to remind you that your warranty on your appliance is about to expire and you need to renew it."

"Thank you for calling, but that appliance is several years old, and I've decided not to renew the warranty," I said.

With a tone of impatience, he responded, "Well, I'm sure your dead husband would want you to renew."

My humor and coping mechanism clicked in and I replied, "Funny you should mention it, but just hours before Paul died he said, 'Honey, whatever you do, don't renew the appliance warranty!'"

There was silence and then John Jones said, "Oh...oh...okay," and hung up.

New churches:

Star Trek—The Next Denomination

Church of the Independent Counsels

—VIA PATTY WOOTEN, SANTA CRUZ, CALIFORNIA

"Let's start at the beginning."

© Jonny Hawkins

The world has always thought that Christians were nuts. The apostle Paul was a fool who knew how nutty it was to follow Jesus. Nuts are a mixed bag. Let's pray for the grace to be fools for Christ and to enjoy being a bit nutty.

—LISA CALDERONE-STEWART, GRAND ISLAND, MAINE

Blessing in Disguise Band

Murphy's Multiple Staff:

Tom is in charge of setting the vision; Dick is in charge of counseling, and Harry handles most of the pulpit duties

© Steve Phelps

FMC member Rev. Jeff Hanna, pastor of First United Methodist Church in Galion, Ohio, reports that a new law in Kentucky, passed in July, 1998, now makes it permissible for a pastor to carry a concealed weapon on church grounds.

The new law, Hanna says jokingly, might open up all kinds of new one-liners for pistol packin' Kentucky pastors. For instance:

• "Repent, or I'll shoot!"

- "I really wish you would reconsider that raise."
- "And now, which points of the sermon do you disagree with?"
- "Who would like to volunteer to teach Sunday school?"
- "I have a really new approach to evangelism. Want to hear it?"
- "Have you seen the latest line of bulletproof robes?"

That's the kind of wacky humor you'd hear at a church that books Hanna's Christian band, Blessing in Disguise (BID). Hanna recently organized his humorous Christian band along with musician-humorists Dave Palmer and Steve Young. He says the band is "a blend of Riders in the Sky, the Smothers Brothers, and the Blues Brothers."

BID offers rock, reggae, blues, folk, gospel, country, and polka music. "If you don't like what you're listening to, stick around—it's about to change," the group tells audiences. Between songs, the group offers jokes and stories.

All of the group's humorous songs are original. "Red Sea Boogie" is a rock number about the people as they boogie across the Red Sea.

"Blues in Eden" is about Adam singing the blues, bemoaning the impact of his sin on future generations.

King Solomon's Tale is "a country number about a great man who had 700 wives...and listened to them instead of God."

"Cowboy for Jesus" is sung with the band wearing cowboy hats and yodeling. A sampling of the lyrics:

> When this life is over, and when my time is done,
>
> May you find me faithful, and lead me to your Son.

And if there's a place for Trigger, up there somewhere with you,

I ask you, Lord, to take him, and not turn him to glue.

The band's humor is wide-ranging. They offer these "Definitions for Computer Illiterate Christians."

Mouse Pad: Where the church mouse lives.

Cursor: The guy down the street you're trying to evangelize.

Browsers: People who visit a church but won't join.

Download: A full dose of the Holy Spirit.

Fatal Error: What happens when you choose not to repent.

Floppy Disk: What happens to your back when you're slain in the Spirit.

Byte: What you might get if you work in the church nursery.

Megabyte: When it really hurts.

"We are really having a great time," says Hanna. "We're making a joyful noise! It's so great to watch people loosen up and have fun in church."

—FOR INFORMATION ON BOOKINGS, WRITE TO: JEFF
HANNA, BID, 615 CENTER ST., GALION, OHIO 44833.

Laughter is the voice of joy that balances the voice of sorrow; laughter is the voice of self-acceptance that opens the heart for acceptance of others; laughter is the voice that reminds us life is a gift meant to be shared with one another from the lodge of the heart in the spirit of joy as well as sorrow.

—KATHY ST. JOHN ANDERSON

"When I was in seminary I did my thesis on the form criticism of I Enoch. I was a teacher's assistant in Ancient Near Eastern Studies. I was conferred as a distinguished fellow in Hebrew Studies. How on earth did I end up as a youth pastor? You tell me."

My Cup Runneth Over, and So Does My Toilet

"We should have fixed the roof before we prayed so hard for rain!"

© Goddard Sherman

Philip Gulley is pastor of Irvington Friends (Quaker) Meeting in Indianapolis. This essay is excerpted from his warm and humorous book Front Porch Tales *(© 1997 by Philip Gulley, and reprinted by permission of Multnomah Publishers, Inc.).*

My sons buy me cards every year at Father's Day. I pay for them, but it's the thought that counts. One year, my card had a star on it. It was actually a bar mitzvah card, but my two-year-old likes stars, so that's the card I got to open at the breakfast table.

We went over to my father's house that afternoon. Most everyone in the family was there because in my family, if you don't show up, you become the topic of conversation. My second cousin wasn't there, so we talked about him. He's a fairly young man but is retired because he's filthy rich. We were glad he wasn't there, since we've been wanting to talk about him for a long time.

None of us like him because he's not only rich, he's happy. We come from a long line of poor people who've been able to endure poverty by believing that rich people are unhappy so a person is better off poor. But my cousin has gone and shattered the myth. He is rich and happy, which makes the rest of us miserable.

We talked about his house. He is married and has no children, but his home has five bathrooms. My grandpa was betting the toilet paper bill alone would break him. I can't imagine having five bathrooms. Our house has one and a half bathrooms, and just keeping those going can be burdensome.

Like the week after Father's Day, when my wife walked into the bathroom and noticed the carpet was damp, and I told her not to worry because it was just humidity. But the next day, the water was squishing up in between our toes. It was less like humidity and more like an underground spring.

Then I noticed that whenever we flushed, water ran down

the back of the tank. I'd never worked on toilets before, but I thought it would build my character, which is what people say when they're too cheap to call a plumber. I worked on it for a few hours before stopping to take a nap. Which is when my wife called a plumber who came and fixed it in five minutes in exchange for a title to our house.

The only comfort I took in all of this was knowing that my cousin has five toilets to take care of, which I think is God's way of teaching him that wealth has its disadvantages. Not that I would know this personally, but I suspect when you're rich you're always wondering why people invite you to parties. Do they like you, or do they like your money? I never wonder why people invite me to parties. It's because they like my wife.

There's a story in the New Testament about a rich man. One day, he asked Jesus what it took to inherit eternal life. Jesus told him to keep the commandments, and when the rich man said he'd done that, Jesus told him to sell all he had and give the money to the poor. And the guy stood around waiting for the punch line. Except Jesus wasn't kidding. The Bible says the man walked away sad, for he was very rich. Personally, I don't think he was rich. I think he was the poorest of the poor.

Let's talk about rich. Every year at Father's Day, I get bar mitzvah cards. I love my wife, and she loves me. Got so many friends our house can't hold them, an icebox full of food, and two toilets. How's that for wealth?

My toilet may runneth over, but so does my cup.

© Ed Sullivan

On Preachers Who Lust After Chicken

"I can't help it; I just love watching him cook his own dinner."

© Marty Bucella

Chicken-lover John Honeycutt, assistant pastor of First Pentecostal Church in Titusville, Florida, says that a number of years ago, "I stopped laughing and ended up in the hospital with physical exhaustion. I simply got too serious. I began to write a collection of humor articles, and overnight my strength was renewed." This article is excerpted from Honeycutt's book Poultry Punch Lines *(© 1996 John Honeycutt; used by permission).*

I've never met a preacher who isn't a chicken-lover, both in the South and in the North, although in the North they don't always admit it.

Why did the preacher cross the road?

To get to the other chicken.

Why didn't the preacher cross the road?

Because the chicken didn't.

What do you call it when a preacher sneaks a piece of chicken before saying grace?

A wing and a prayer.

Why did the preacher believe that God was not prejudiced?

He made chickens out of both white and dark meat.

What do you call a preacher who claims to be a vegetarian?

A liar.

Why did the preacher start a new ministry for chickens?

He knew that so many were being battered.

Why do most theologians believe that chicken was served at the Lord's supper?

What else would you serve a bunch of preachers who get together to eat?

Why did David become king?

He could kill two birds with one stone.

What is the dream of every chicken strutting the earth?

Having a preacher for lunch.

Why did the chicken always walk behind the preacher?

He knew that the minister was a backstabber.

What do preachers and the Lord have in common?

They both notice when a bird falls to the ground.

Why did a raven, and not a chicken, feed the prophet Elijah?

The Lord wanted the bird to return.

What does a preacher call a small offering?

Chicken-feed.

What is one reason chicken is served at church picnics?

Preachers find it easier to hide and take home a chicken thigh in their sports coats as compared to a slab of steak or a big round burger.

Why did the preacher get mad?

He heard that someone had kicked the bucket.

SOME WAYS A PREACHER CAN CATCH A CHICKEN:

- Place a fake grave marker with Colonel Sanders's name on it in their front yard and when the chickens gather around to spit on it, nab 'em.
- Advertise a shelter for battered chickens.
- Act really scared and then they will think you are a chicken.

SOME REASONS WHY PREACHERS EAT CHICKEN LATE AT NIGHT:

- In order to get one last taste just in case the Rapture takes place sometime in the night.
- Because they don't believe in eating leftovers the next day.
- Because they don't want to be wasteful and throw away perfectly good food.
- God told him to "arise and eat."
- Because he is in the mood to chew out someone in his flock.

THINGS A CHICKEN WOULD LIKE TO DO TO A PREACHER:

- Make him sleep in aluminum foil while in a sauna for one night.
- Every fifteen minutes, spray him in the face with a baster of human sweat.
- Invite him to a picnic and make him sit in the middle of a table while twenty chickens stare at him.
- Make him cross the road and explain, in detail, why he did.
- Bake him into a potpie.
- Secretly take the preacher into a remote barn to fight another preacher, and cash in on it.

"Welcome to the *real* Moral Majority, Bixley."

If God the Father saw fit to clothe His Son in a human body, that makes the body sacred, so when we take care of that body by diet, exercise, prayer, laughter—especially laughter at ourselves—we give glory to God.

—REV. TOM WALSH, SCOTTSDALE, ARIZONA

Self-Esteem Goeth Before a Fall

"With sex education, self-esteem, multiculturalism, self-awareness, computer studies, and touchy feely, I'm not going to have time for reading, writing and arithmetic. That's where you, as parents, come in…"

© Harley L. Schwadron

Nobody should have been surprised by the latest results of the Third International Mathematics and Science Study, because American students have been doing badly on international tests for decades.

American twelfth graders fell below the international average in general mathematics and general science. In advanced mathematics, our students were tied for last place, and in physics they had sole possession of last place.

American public schools are indulging themselves in all sorts of fads and psychobabble, including "self-esteem." American students led the world in one department: "self-esteem." As in previous international tests, American students had the highest perception of how well they had done. This would be comical if it were not so tragic.

—THOMAS SOWELL, COLUMNIST, THE *DETROIT NEWS*

At Case Western Reserve University in Cleveland, psychology Prof. Roy Baumeister studied the personalities of several hundred criminals and concluded that the criminals, rather than suffering from low self-esteem, had gigantic egos.

Dr. Baumeister suggested that what is needed in American society is less self-esteem and more humility.

He asked: "Does anyone really think that the cause of world peace would be served if we boosted Saddam Hussein's self-esteem?"

The difference between self-esteem and self-respect is night and day. A person with "high self-esteem" thinks highly of himself.

A person growing in self-respect understands that he is an imperfect being who was given the gift of life in order to serve.

A person with high self-esteem thinks he is deserving; therefore, he is ungrateful. A person growing in self-respect thinks he is undeserving; therefore, he is grateful.

—JOHN ROSEMOND, FAMILY COUNSELOR,
CHARLOTTE, NORTH CAROLINA

A LESSON IN HUMILITY

As a new young pastor, I worried about how people would receive me. One day I went out to visit a new member. Climbing the steps to the front door, I noticed the newspaper on the welcome mat. I picked it up, ready to hand it over when the door opened.

A little girl answered the door, took one look at me, and yelled over her shoulder, "Hey Mom, it's the newspaper boy."

That quickly put things in perspective for me, and I never again wondered about my image.

—REV. JERRY ROBBINS, LUTHERAN CAMPUS PASTOR,
WEST VIRGINIA UNIVERSITY,
MORGANTOWN, WEST VIRGINIA

A nineteenth-century poem:

> Ten thousand reformers like so many moles,
> Have plowed all the Bible and cut it in holes;
> And each has his church at the end of his trace,
> Built up as he thinks of the subjects of grace.

—AUTHOR UNKNOWN

Don't hang a dismal picture on the wall, and don't have gloom in your conversations. Don't be a cynic and disconsolate. Don't bewail and bemoan. Omit the negative propositions. Nerve us with incessant affirmatives. Don't waste yourself in rejection or bark against the bad, but chant the beauty of the good. Set down nothing that will not help somebody.

—RALPH WALDO EMERSON

TEDDY ROOSEVELT BEAT DEPRESSION
BY RIDING AND NOT LOOKING BACK

As a child and as a young man, Theodore Roosevelt suffered from asthma and bouts with depression. His depression deepened after both his young wife and his mother died from illnesses on the same night.

His father, a devout Christian, advised him to keep the faith, go West, build up his body with lots of exercise, and help others less well-to-do than he was. Roosevelt went to South Dakota and became a cowboy.

"Black care rarely sits behind a rider whose pace is fast enough," Roosevelt later said.

His depressions dissipated, and Roosevelt returned to become one of America's wittiest and most energetic presidents, however controversial.

© Harley L. Schwadron

Don't live in the past. Don't live in the future.
This is the moment God has given us to be useful.

—FULTON SHEEN

To forgive heals the wound; to forget heals the scar.

—P. T. BARNUM

In Praise of Laughter

© Ed Sullivan

When the Fellowship of Merry Christians was organized in 1986, the distinguished monastic historian and theologian, Dom Jean Leclerq, OSB, a monk of the Benedictine Abbey of Clervaux in Luxembourg, sent us a photograph of an unusual wooden crucifix dating from the twelfth century. There is a gentle smile on the face of the crucified Christ on the cross, hinting of the joy of the coming Resurrection.

The "smiling crucifix of the twelfth century" was found in the Cistercian monastery of Lérins in southern France. The monastery of Lérins was founded in the early fifth century, and one of its early abbots, Hilary (which means "cheerful" or "merry" in Greek) was later canonized.

The monastery was famous for its troubadours and writers. St. Patrick lived there for a time before going to Ireland.

One can only speculate whether the smiling crucifix of Lérins might have inspired, centuries later, the Lebanese poet Kahlil Gibran's vision of a crucified Christ smiling from the cross upon His mother, Mary.

In his book *Jesus the Son of Man,* Gibran wrote: "And we came close to her (Mary), and she said to us, 'Even in death He smiles. He has conquered. I would indeed be the mother of a conqueror.'"

Leclercq also contributed the following article, "In Praise of Laughter," to *The Joyful Noiseletter* a few years before he went to the Lord at a ripe old age:

Many of the sayings of those early monks, who were known as the Desert Fathers and who were renowned for their humor, were said with a smile or with tongue-in-cheek. In fact several of these monks, as well as other saints, were actually called by names meaning "the smiling one."

"Hilary," "Hilarion," for example. Hilary, bishop of Poitiers, was one of the greatest theologians of early times.

Hilarity means the capacity for smiling and laughing, and is both a gift of the Holy Spirit and a virtue to acquire, to hold onto, and to preach about. And it is such, first of all, because it is an attribute of God.

The theme of the hilarity of God has been developed in other places, and the final achievement of those who shared in it most fully was "to die with a smile," as it is written of many of the saints.

God laughs and humans laugh; when God in Jesus took a human nature, He also became able to laugh as well as to suffer and to die.

He was even able to reconcile, in His life and in His death—His supreme act of love—a deep suffering with a joy which has been represented in crucifixes that are to be found in monasteries of the early Gothic period; these are known as "the smiling Christs."

Among others, there is a smiling Christ on the cross dating from the 12th century in the Cistercian monastery of Lérins in southern France. In monastic writings of the same period, beautiful texts can be found which try to express, if not explain, this paradoxical mystery: "Was He joyful or sad? Let us say He was both at once."

St. Bernard of Clairvaux often made use of words, images and ideas connected with hilarity. After praising the smiling and laughter of an Irish saint of his times, St. Malachy, Bernard declared: "What a perfect gift!"

All this leads to what he called a "playful devotion" (*iucunda*, using a Latin word from which the English word "joke" derives), and this embraces the divine and human playfulness, which is how the monastic life ought to be lived out. As St. Bernard put it in one of his sermons to his monks: "Let everything be filled with the fervor of the Spirit and with playful devotion."

Prayers for Laughter

From somber, serious, sullen saints, save us, O Lord. Lord, hear our prayer.

—Teresa of Avila (1582)

May our mouths be filled with laughter, and our tongues with singing.

—Charles H. Spurgeon (1892), English Baptist pastor

© Wendell W. Simons

The Healing Power of Holy Hilarity

FMC member William Griffin is "a walking miracle," according to his pastor, Rev. David R. Francoeur, former rector of Christ Episcopal Church in Valdosta, Georgia.

When he was a colonel in the air force eighteen years ago,

Griffin was involved in a terrible accident overseas. He was in a coma for a long time.

"When he emerged from the coma in the early days of his recovery, he told me he couldn't communicate in any form but laughter," Reverend Francoeur said. "He couldn't speak, and his eyesight was poor, but he laughed a lot. I find this remarkable and told him that this is a sign of the healing work of the Holy Spirit. Today he is almost fully recovered."

Reverend Francoeur added: "The other day I was complaining to him about how God is so slow in answering prayer in comparison to the speed with which I think He should move. 'Why does God move so slow?' I asked him.

"'Because He's older than you are,' he replied."

© Ed Sullivan

I saw the Lord scorn the devil's malice and reduce his powerlessness to nothing, and He wills that we do the same thing. On account of this sight, I laughed loud and long, which made those who were around me laugh, too, and their laughter was a pleasure to me. Then I thought I would like all my fellow Christians to have seen what I saw, for then they should all laugh with me. For I understood that we may laugh, comforting ourselves and rejoicing in God that the devil has been overcome.

—DAME JULIAN OF NORWICH, FOURTEENTH-CENTURY ENGLISH MYSTIC

The Fun Nun

"Theology has nothing to do with it, Mrs. Westfall. If I bless your lottery ticket, I'll have to bless everybody's."

"The Fun Nun," a.k.a. Sr. Mary Christelle Macaluso, RSM, Ph.D., OFN, spreads joy and laughter from her base at the College of Saint Mary in Omaha, Nebraska.

A popular speaker and consulting editor to *The Joyful Noiseletter*, the Fun Nun searched the Bible for verses reflecting the theme of joy, and came up with an uplifting new book, entitled *God Knows Best About Joy.*

Each Bible verse is accompanied by a short "reflection to lift up the heart." Here are some samples:

> This is the day the LORD has made. We will rejoice and be glad in it. (Psalm 118:24, NLT)

Reflection: "A-n-o-t-h-e-r day... Do you rejoice or do you groan? Celebrate life! Greet each day with joy in your heart!"

> Your eyes light up your inward being. A pure eye lets sunshine into your soul.... If you are filled with light within, with no dark corners, then your face will be radiant too, as though a floodlight is beamed upon you. (Luke 11:34-36)
>
> A fool's fun is being bad, a wise man's fun is being wise. (Proverbs 10:23)

Reflection: "So much evil is done in the name of 'just having fun.' May all your fun be a delight in God's sight."

> The dawn and sunset shout for joy! (Psalm 65:8)

Reflection: "The psalmist is telling you to imitate nature—join its A.M. and P.M. shouts of joy and praise. Try it!"

> A happy face means a glad heart; a sad face means a breaking heart. (Proverbs 15:13)

Reflection: "Since the mind affects the body and the body affects the mind, you can become a happier person by putting on a smile. Pass that smile on to others."

But may the godly man exult. May he rejoice and be
merry. (Psalm 68:3)

Reflection: "Are you a godly man or woman? If so, get ready to
make merry!"

When a man is gloomy, everything seems to go wrong;
when he is cheerful, everything seems right! (Proverbs
15:15)

Reflection: "You are in control of your attitude. You may not
be able to change some events in your life, but you can change
your reaction to them. The next time you drop something on the
floor, thank God for the opportunity to exercise!"

The whole earth has seen God's salvation of his people.
That is why the earth breaks out in praise to God, and
sings for utter joy! (Psalm 98:3-4)

Reflection: "Come join the choir! Practice times: Monday
through Sunday 12 A.M.–11:59 P.M."

Always be full of joy in the Lord; I say it again, rejoice!
(Philippians 4:4)

Reflection: "This message is so important the apostle Paul
felt he had to say it twice!"

Cheerful givers are the ones God prizes. (2 Corinthians 9:7)

Reflection: "Give with a smile on your face and joy in your
heart! The size of the gift doesn't matter, but the thought behind

it does. Sometimes the greatest gift is your time. Be one of God's prizes."

> It is a wonderful thing to be alive! If a person lives to be
> very old, let him rejoice in every day of life, but let him also
> remember that eternity is far longer, and that everything
> down here is futile in comparison. (Ecclesiastes 11:7-8)

Reflection: "May you grow old gracefully because you do so joyfully. Life is too short to spend it being grouchy!"

© M. Larry Zanco

Can This Be Jesus?

"What do you guys think—should we wake up the Master?"

The following story comes from Cal Samra, editor of The Joyful Noiseletter.

A story is told about Abraham Lincoln that he once was shown a painting in the home of a friend, and asked what he thought of it.

"I think he is a good painter in that he observes the Lord's commandments," Lincoln replied. "He hath not made to himself the likeness of anything that is in heaven above, nor that is in the earth beneath, nor that is in the waters under the earth."

The same might be said about many of the representations of Jesus currently being printed by publications and publishers of all denominations.

Many of these paintings can be variously described as ugly, grim, morbid, depressive, joyless, gruesome, macabre, bizarre, wimpy, uninspiring, tasteless.

Gazing upon any one of them, one wonders: Can this be Jesus? Can this be the Messiah, the God of love, the God of joy, the God of mercy, the God of courage, the Prince of peace, the Healer of depressives, the Great Physician, the Holy Mighty, the Holy Immortal, the Savior of the world?

Can this be the Jesus who said: "Whenever you fast, do not put on a gloomy face as the hypocrites do" (Matthew 6:16, NASB)?

Can this be the Jesus who promised His disciples shortly before He was crucified: "I have told you this so that my joy may be in you and that your joy may be complete" (John 15:11, NIV)?

We know that Jesus attracted children to Him. Would a Jesus who looked like these artists' representations attract children, or scare them away? We also know that Jesus attracted the sick and the depressed to Him. Would a Jesus who looked like these artists' representations attract the sick and depressed?

I think they'd be scared away.

Image may not be everything, but if the devil is still determined to sabotage the Christian faith, one major strategy would be to enlist artists to distort Jesus' image and to make Him so unappealing that people would be discouraged from following Him.

An Italian Dominican, Tommaso Campanella (1568-1639) made this appeal to the painters of his day: "Paint Christ not dead but risen, with His foot set in scorn on the split rock with which they sought to hold Him down! Paint Him the Conqueror of death! Paint Him the Lord of life! Paint Him as what He is, the irresistible Victor who, tested to the uttermost, has proved Himself in very deed mighty to save!"

Today, there is an incredible scarcity of good resurrection art. (*The Risen Christ by the Sea* by Jack Jewell and *I Am the Resurrection* by Deborah L. Zeller are exceptions. Both of these increasingly popular prints are available through the FMC catalog.) There is a great need for a revival in religious art.

This presents both a challenge and an opportunity to contemporary religious artists. We hope and pray that they will rise to the occasion.

I have a friend who radiates joy, not because his life is easy, but because he habitually recognizes God's presence in the midst of all human suffering, his own as well as others. My friend's joy is contagious.

The more I am with him, the more I catch glimpses of the sun shining through the clouds. While my friend always spoke about the sun, I kept speaking about the clouds, until one day I realized that it was the sun that allowed me to see the clouds.

Those who keep speaking about the sun while walking

under a cloudy sky are messengers of hope, the true saints of our day.

—Henri Nouwen

The Gospel of Christ's resurrection fills the heart with joy! A triumphant love song is already beginning.

—Catherine Doherty

"The worst thing about being married to a prophet besides washing his sackcloth is the fact that you can never throw him a surprise party."

© Dik LaPine

How to Celebrate "Holy Humor Sunday"

"Agatha always gets a bit carried away on the 'He Arose' part."

© Karl R. Kraft

"Holy Humor Sunday," the Sunday after Easter, has become a tradition at the United Methodist Church of Mantua, New Jersey—a party to celebrate the resurrection of Jesus.

FMC member Rev. Dr. Karl R. Kraft reports that Holy Humor Sunday was clearly identified on the front of the church bulletin.

The organist began with the prelude, "Just Put on a Happy Face." The choir then processed into the sanctuary carrying balloons and singing, "I've Got That Joy, Joy, Joy, Joy." The balloons were placed behind the altar rail.

There were several "holy humor responses," from a psalm or hymn about joy and praise.

The congregation sang "If You're Happy and You Know It" while stomping their feet.

The children's anthem was "Scratch Your Neighbor's Back," and Reverend Kraft said, "They had the whole congregation shaking hands and scratching each other's backs."

Reverend Kraft walked through the congregation giving them an Easter "pep talk." The pastor invited the congregation to sing and shout out whatever they felt would make them joyful on Easter, such as "Praise the Lord!" or "Thanks be to God!"

A small preschool boy shouted: "I want to go home!"

Kraft gave up his sermon time to members of the congregation, who were invited to share their jokes and short stories. Those who didn't have a joke or one-liner "were invited to choose one from a box of shtick." (Kraft had clipped out a variety of jokes and one-liners from various sources and placed them in a wooden treasure chest.)

All of the ushers wore colorful "Cat in the Hat" hats. They took them off and used them to collect the offering.

Many people took Kraft's suggestion that they come dressed in splashy, bright, or comical attire.

"It was a great experience for us all." says Kraft. "I noticed that even the people with heavy concerns—deaths in the family, personal problems, disharmony in relationships—left the service smiling. "Thank you, FMC, for reviving this ancient practice that has so much to offer us today."

Trinity Presbyterian Church in Williamsport, Indiana, also celebrated Holy Humor Sunday with a special service led by Rev. Patricia Kuhs, according to Candy Hunter, the choir director.

"There are those who just won't believe that Christians can celebrate in such a joyous fashion." said Hunter.

The bulletin included a "Litany of Joy."

Our church shared again the joy of worship on "Holy Hilarity Sunday" (the Sunday after Easter), helped along by some jokes from *The Joyful Noiseletter*.

Years ago, when our daughter, Connie, was a teenager, she looked forward to the Easter dawn service more than Christmas. To this day, she still drags her three boys out of bed in the wee hours of Easter morning to once again experience the miracle of the Resurrection. They ask, "Why, Mom?" Her answer is, "We are Easter people!"

—REV. FREDERICK L. HAYNES, PRINCE OF PEACE
LUTHERAN CHURCH, RUSSELL SPRINGS, KENTUCKY

Just before Easter, a Sunday school teacher at Bethany Lutheran Church in Brodhead, Wisconsin, was telling the story of Barabbas to a group of preschool children. A little girl interrupted him: "I have barabbits at home!"

—VIA PASTOR DALE L. RADKE,
MILWAUKEE, WISCONSIN

"I was slapping high-fives because it was Palm Sunday."

A JOYFUL FAITH NEEDS BALANCE

"Good Friday Christians," who tend to wallow in morose reminders of Jesus hanging on a cross, sometimes never allow themselves to realize that joy is meant to follow sorrow.

On the other hand, "Palm-Sunday-to-Easter Christians" choose to skip from Palm Sunday's triumphant entry of Jesus into Jerusalem right into Easter Sunday, pretending the passion story of Jesus never happened. These Christians may never allow themselves to realize that without sorrow, joy can be shallow and brittle.

Can we find a balance somewhere in between these two positions?

A distraught young woman once complained to her grand-mother. "In life's pilgrimage, the bags get awfully heavy some-times."

The wise grandmother replied, "Yes, but laughter is the porter who helps us carry the bags."

I hear many Christians mouth the words of a joyful faith, but I miss seeing the acts of a joyful faith from a great many of these same persons.

Easter Day is coming! I hope you invite laughter and joy to carry your baggage on Easter Day.

—FMC MEMBER REV. PAUL R. GRAVES,
SANDPOINT, IDAHO.

© Steve Phelps

After authoring twenty-seven books in his lifetime, *The Joyful Noiseletter* consulting editor Sherwood Eliot Wirt, a longtime associate of Billy Graham, finally got a bestseller at the age of eighty-eight. In his new best-selling book, *Jesus: Man of Joy* (Harvest House Publishers), Wirt wrote:

"The secret of Jesus was—and is—His inner joy. Many intimations in the New Testament lead us to believe that while in our midst, Jesus had a cheerful disposition and a merry heart.... In a hundred places the Bible tells us that the message of salvation in Christ is a message of love bathed in joy. The very word *gospel* means 'good news, glad tidings.'

"Do a little surfing through the Bible on your own, looking for joy. What a wealth of joyful expression!"

> Joy is something released from within, not acquired from without... Whether it has been placed there by circumstances, other people or our own response to the trials of life, let us roll away the stone that would keep God-given joy entombed within us, and tap the power of the resurrection of our Lord. Easter joy!
>
> —CLAIRE M. BASTIEN, *THE CHURCH WORLD*, BRUNSWICK, MAINE

What Your Doctor's Office Will Be Like in A.D. 2010

"The A.M.A. now says laughter is the best medicine."

© Harley L. Schwadron

Patty Wooten of Santa Cruz, California, a registered nurse, humorist, and clown who often appears as "Nancy Nurse," thinks too many people suffer from "terminal seriousness." Her book Compassionate Laughter: Jest for your Health *(Commune-A-Key Publishing) is a journey into the wacky world of therapeutic humor. The book includes these fanciful musings by Wooten on what it will be like to visit a doctor in the year A.D. 2010 (© 1996 Patty Wooten. Reprinted with permission).*

Imagine. The year is 2010, and therapeutic humor is now accepted as a complementary treatment in healthcare. Today you have an appointment to see your physician because of a persistent headache.

You arrive at the doctor's office, tired from the day's work and anxious about the possible cause of your headache. After all, your father had a brain tumor removed when he was about your age.

As you enter the office, the receptionist smiles, welcomes you, and offers you a small tape player with headphones and a choice of comedy audiocassettes to entertain you while you wait. You choose your favorite comedian and settle back. Your anxiety and fatigue begin to melt, and you begin to relax. Soon you are laughing.

You are called into the examination room where a bulletin board of cartoons keeps you amused until the physician arrives. In a few minutes, the doctor enters the room. The doctor offers to share a few new jokes, and soon you are both laughing together.

You relax a bit more and a sense of connection and trust begins to build between you and the doctor. After a thorough examination, the doctor explains some concerns and requests that you complete a CAT scat within a week.

Later that week, you arrive at the hospital's outpatient clinic and register with the clerk. You notice a box full of toys. The clerk invites you to play with them while your chart is being prepared. Soon you have several windup toys moving and hopping around the desktop. You are both smiling as the clerk hands you the chart and directs you to the radiology department.

The waiting room is crowded with people awaiting radiation therapy appointments, as well as those scheduled for diagnostic procedures. Some small children are sitting near their worried parents.

Suddenly, you hear music, a perky little tune created by a ukulele and a penny whistle. Everyone turns toward the music and starts to smile as two clowns enter the waiting room. They move about greeting people, introducing their puppets and blowing bubbles which the children try to catch on their noses. Some people receive a "clown nose transplant," others receive colorful stickers.

After ten minutes, almost everyone in the room is laughing. Some are amused by the comical antics of the clowns, others comforted by the delight shining from the eyes of these sick children.

After your CAT scan and subsequent angiogram are determined to be normal, your physician concludes that your headaches are most likely caused by the unrelieved tension, pressures, and deadlines at your workplace. The doctor asks that you meet with the office nurse for some stress-management training.

You expect to be given the same information about relaxation, exercise, and diet that you've heard before, but this time is different. Your nurse talks about the health benefits of humor and laughter.

After you answer many questions about your preference for humor styles and artists, the nurse creates a list of humorous books, audio and videotapes and articles about humor, all available from the Laughter Library at the hospital or the humor section of the local community library. You receive a list of humorous videotapes for rent at a local video outlet.

You remember how relaxed you felt each time you laughed through the tensions of the last week, how the comedy tapes, cartoons, toys, and clowns all brought welcome relief from the stress of the moment.

You make a promise to yourself: a promise to protect your health and well-being by seeking and responding to moments of humor and laughter. *Jest for your health!*

"We gather today to honor our youth pastor who died last Saturday from what the doctors are determining to be an overdose of cholesterol from eating too many pizzas."

© Dik LaPine

Turning ninety-five, comedian Bob Hope told *TV Guide* the secret to his longevity: "Laughter is it. Laughter is therapy—an instant vacation."

Acknowledgments and Permissions

We are most grateful to all of the people who contributed jokes, anecdotes, and stories to this book.

The editors of *The Joyful Noiseletter* diligently sought to track down the original source for a joke or anecdote and give due credit in this book. When we were unable to determine the original source, we acknowledged the person who passed on the item to *The Joyful Noiseletter*.

We also thank and salute the following individuals, authors, and publishers for their assistance and permission to reprint the named materials:

The Anglican Digest for permission to reprint "Report of the Search Committee."

Rev. Ron Birk, a Lutheran pastor, and LangMarc Publishing in San Antonio, Texas, for permission to reprint a sampling from his book, *You Might Be in a Country Church If...* (© 1998 Ron Birk).

Lutheran Pastor Denny J. Brake of Raleigh, North Carolina, for "Prescription for the Blues."

C. Justin Clements, director of the Office of Stewardship and Development, in the Catholic Diocese of Evansville, Indiana, for the entertaining "Hymn Game."

Lois Blanchard Eades of Dickson, Tennessee, for sharing some of her "Biblimericks" and contributing her poem "For Better or Woof."

Cy Eberhart, a United Church of Christ chaplain in Salem, Oregon, for "A Young Pastor's First Hospital Call," from his book, *Burnt Offerings — Parables for 20th Century Christians* (© Cy Eberhart).

Steve Feldman of Jefferson City, Missouri, for passing along the story "In the Beginning."

Randy Fishell, of Seattle, Washington, associate editor of *Guide*, and Review and Herald Publishing Association, for "Moving Testimony of a Youth Pastor," an adaptation from his book *Hair Today, Gone Tomorrow* (© 1996 Review and Herald Publishing Association. Used by permission.)

Rev. David R. Francoeur, for permission to print his article "Tips to Help Pastors Buy a Used Car" (© David R. Francoeur).

George and Peggy Goldtrap of Happy Talk, Int'l, Ormond-by-the-Sea, Florida, for their numerous humorous contributions.

Rev. Paul R. Graves of Sandpoint, Idaho, for "A Joyful Faith Needs Balance."

Phil Gulley, pastor of Irvington Friends (Quaker) Meeting in Indianapolis, and Multnomah Publishers, Inc. for "My Cup Runneth Over, and So Does My Toilet," from his book *Front Porch Tales* (© 1997 by Philip Gulley. Reprinted by permission of Multnomah Publishers, Inc.).

Rev. Jeff Hanna, pastor of First United Methodist Church in Galion, Ohio, for the one-liners and humorous offerings from his Blessings in Disguise Band.

Rev. Jeff Hayes, "Pastor Pun," of Sioux Falls, South Dakota, for sharing a sampling from his collection of amusing church signs.

Liz Curtis Higgs of Louisville, Kentucky, and Thomas Nelson Publishers, Nashville, Tennessee, for permission to reprint "Bifocals Can Make Life More Fun After the Big 4-0" from Liz's book, *Forty Reasons Why Life Is More Fun After the Big 4-0* (© 1997 Liz Curtis Higgs).

Rev. John Honeycutt, assistant pastor of First Pentecostal Church in Titusville, Florida, for permission to reprint excerpts from his book, *Poultry Punch Lines* (© 1996 John Honeycutt).

Rev. Warren J. Keating, pastor of First Presbyterian Church, Derby, Kansas, and *Net Results* for permission to reprint his joyful article "Fostering the Fun Factor" from the June 1998 *Net Results*. All rights reserved. *Net Results* is a monthly journal of "New Ideas in Church Vitality" published in Lubbock, Texas. (Reverend Keating is now rejoicing in heaven.)

Rev. Dr. Karl R. Kraft, pastor of the United Methodist Church of Mantua, New Jersey, for sharing his congregation's joyful celebration of "Holy Humor Sunday."

Dom Jean Leclerq, OSB, a former Benedictine monk of Clervaux, Luxembourg, now with the Lord, for his article, "In Praise of Laughter."

Rev. Paul Lintern, associate pastor of First English Lutheran Church in Mansfield, Ohio, for "Things That Spell Trouble at a Wedding" (© Paul Lintern).

Sr. Mary Christelle Macaluso, RSM, Ph.D., OFN, aka "The Fun Nun," at the College of Saint Mary in Omaha, Nebraska, for the joyful Bible verses and reflections from her new book, *God Knows Best About Joy* (© 1998 Sr. Mary Christelle Macaluso. Fun Nun Books).

Tom Mullen of Richmond, Indiana, and Friends United Press for permission to reprint "On Giving Devotions" from his book *Where Two or Three Are Gathered Someone Spills the Milk* (© Tom Mullen).

David A. Robb of Dalton, Georgia, and The Hymn Society in the United States for permission to reprint "Ode to the Third Stanza" (© David A. Robb).

Dr. Rex Russell, M.D., a radiologist in Fort Smith, Arkansas, and Regal Books, Ventura, California, for excerpts from his book *What the Bible Says About Healthy Living* (© 1996 Rex Russell, M.D.).

Barbara Shlemon Ryan, of Brea, California, for contributing the "Prayer of a Mellowing Nun" by an anonymous seventeenth-century nun.

Kay Dekalb Smith, of Brentwood, Tennessee, for inspiring the article on "The Carol Burnett of Christian Comedy."

Rev. James L. Snyder, minister with the Christian and Missionary Alliance, currently serving the First Alliance Church in Ocala, Florida, for permission to print "Invasion of the Cucumbers."

Rev. Chuck Terrill, minister of Haverhill Christian Church in Augusta, Kansas, and Morris Publishing, for "I Heard an Angel's Voice" from his book *Hope and Hilarity: Positive Stories of Faith, Family and Fun,* illustrated by Bryan Clark (© 1996 Chuck Terrill).

Nazarene Pastor Dr. Stan Toler of Bethany, Oklahoma, and Honor Books for permission to use a sampling from his book *Minister's Little Instruction Book* (© Stan Toler).

Ann Weeks of Louisville, Kentucky, for permission to reprint "The Appliance Man Ringeth" from her book *She Laughs and the World Laughs with Her* (© Ann Weeks).

Rev. David E. Welsh, senior minister at Central Christian Church in Ocala, Florida, for permission to reprint "Roy Rogers's Top Ten."

Dr. Paul R. Welter, a counselor in Kearney, Nebraska, and a University of Nebraska professor, for permission to reprint "Growing Down" from his class "Learning from Children."

Sherwood Eliot Wirt of Poway, California, eighty-eight-year-old author of the best-selling book *Jesus: Man of Joy* (Harvest House Publishers) for his friendship and wise counsel through the years.

Patty Wooten, RN, aka "Nancy Nurse," of Santa Cruz, California, for her numerous humorous contributions and for "What Your Doctor's Office Will Be Like in 2010 A.D." from her book *Compassionate Laughter: Jest for Your Health*, Commune-A-Key Publishing, Salt Lake City, Utah (© 1996 Patty Wooten. Reprinted with permission).

Index of Subjects

Index of Contributors
and Resources

About the Authors

୭

Cal Samra is a former newspaper and wire-service reporter. He worked for the *New York Herald Tribune*, the *Newark Evening News*, Associated Press, the *Ann Arbor News*, and the *Battle Creek Enquirer*. He is the author of *The Joyful Christ: The Healing Power of Humor*.

Rose Samra has been involved in music and intercession ministries. She has worked for Christian education, health, and agricultural organizations.

The Samras are coauthors of the two best-selling books, *Holy Humor* and *More Holy Humor*. They live in Portage, Michigan, and have three sons: Luke, Matthew, and Paul.

The Fellowship of
Merry Christians

For information about the Fellowship of Merry Christians and
The Joyful Noiseletter, Please call toll-free 1-800-877-2757 from
8:00 a.m. to 5:00 p.m. EST, Monday–Friday, or write:FMC, PO
Box 895, Portage, MI 49081-0895. E-mail: JoyfulNZ@aol.com.
Visit FMC's Web site: www.joyfulnoiseletter.com.

A NOTE FROM THE EDITORS

This book was selected by the Book and Inspirational Media Division of the company that publishes *Guideposts,* a monthly magazine filled with true stories of people's adventures in faith.

Guideposts is not sold on the newsstand. It's available by subscription only. And subscribing is easy. All you have to do is write to Guideposts, 39 Seminary Hill Road, Carmel, New York 10512. When you subscribe, each month you can count on receiving exciting new evidence of God's presence, His guidance and His limitless love for all of us.

Guideposts is also available on the Internet by accessing our home page on the World Wide Web at www.guideposts.org. Send prayer requests to our Monday morning Prayer Fellowship. Read stories from recent issues of our magazines, *Guideposts, Angels on Earth, Clarity, Guideposts for Kids,* and *Guideposts for Teens,* and follow our popular book of devotionals, *Daily Guideposts.* Excerpts from some of our best-selling books are also available.